Home Economics:
How to Run the Whole House, Budget, and Garden

By Kate Singh

Author of *One Paycheck and a Housewife* and *The Frugal Life*

Blog: www.coffeewithkate.blog
YouTube Channel: Coffee With Kate

Edited by Perla Thornwood
Cover Design by James at www.goonwrite.com

Table of Contents

Chapter 1

The House Manager

I had spent a weekend pondering my duties and those of my fellow homemakers and was inspired to write this article for my blog. I shall share it to start us all off because it is one of those rare moments that I really captured the life of those of us in this field.

My Job as a House Manager

I love waiting in dental and doctors' offices. I am the one person who has no problem when the staff are running late (if I have no children, that is). I bring a book and enjoy that quiet time, amen!

The other day I waited my turn for a teeth cleaning and enjoyed some time reading *Introduction to Home Economics: Gentle Instruction to Find Joy in Christian Homemaking* by Mrs. Sharon White. The entry was about a homemaker's worth in dollars. We have read many articles on this and I have even discussed this in my videos before.

We add up the salary of a driver, cook, maid,

secretary, teacher, butler, nanny, etc. We calculate what it would cost to pay a gardener to mow the lawns, the amount to pay a dog walker, the costs of daycare, and a part-time house cleaner. Don't forget to add up takeout, delivery, restaurants, Starbucks, and the deli down the block from work.

But I've got a new spin on this old topic. When others ask you what you do all day, or tell you to get a job, put the kids in school, and get on with it (as if you may be lazing in fields of clover and letting the children run wild in the streets while others are actually being productive members of society), you tell them that you are a house manager and your boss would become hysterical at the loss of one of his (or her) most valuable employees.

After all, you are running that small world your family lives in, which you call "home."

No need to get up in arms. As Jesus said, "Forgive them for they know not what they do." Right? I've had rude people come on my YouTube channel and say to me that I need to put my children in school and go back to work. Guess what I do with those people? I report them as either hate speech or harassment. Yessir! I ain't messin' around, people!

Now, let's get this straight. I'm no Martha Stewart or queen of organization and I certainly can't hold a candle to the home cooks out there making fancy jellies and stews, but I work on it daily.

I get lazy. I buy and bake premade foods. My house is shameful at times. I can't fold worth a darn, even with all the Marie Kondo shows on how to fold. My skill set makes my friends' eyes roll. It makes them tell me it's too painful to watch.

Deep cleaning is a new thing for me. I have been

known to do chores in my pjs. In fact, I find them quite suitable for daywear (only at home though). Not much about my home is Instagram worthy and few of my ideas are Pinterest ready.

Despite a list of faults and shortcomings, I am a wonderful mother and homemaker most of the time (a good portion of the time...frequently)!

I am the House Manager! It's the new title I gave myself today after a few days of pondering this whole topic. I should be earning a good and solid $60,000 a year with benefits, paid holidays and vacations, weekends off, plus much more.

We know this is not realistic, so I will forgo weekends and take my work with me (a.k.a. family) on holidays and vacations. However, I insist on time off in the form of a movie alone in a dark theater with Milk Duds and delicious, buttery popcorn, especially when the next Star Wars movie comes out. This is non-negotiable.

I will also add to the list (since I don't get evenings or nights off) that a gym membership at my favorite racquet club is added as well as some extra cash now and then for thrifting.

Oh, alright! Forget the $60,000 annual salary, but the gym membership, movie night and extra cash now and then are non-negotiable! Period!

Now that I've at least evaluated my worth, let's see what I offer, shall we?

I manage the house, as the title suggests. This includes work in the following areas: administrative, maintenance, cleaning, organization, and financial affairs. I make appointments and make sure subjects arrive at those appointments, be they medical, dental, chiropractic, and so on. I sign children up for independent study and an outdoor forest school. I retrieve, complete, and submit necessary paperwork and plan out classes, schedules, curriculum, and order proper materials. There is also homeschooling where I'm responsible for the education and development of two humans so that when they go out into the world, they are prepared on many levels. It is my duty to be sure that they are well-mannered, compassionate, and become valuable community members.

As for the housework, there is daily cleaning, weekly all-over cleaning, seasonal deep cleaning, and the big chores I save for yearly self-torture. There are rooms that need organizing of clothes, kitchen tools, bathroom supplies, as well as gadget control. Cleaning solutions need to be made or purchased. Sometimes repairs and maintenance need to be scheduled with professionals. I make those appointments and make sure that things are done in a timely manner.

There are kitchen gardens, fruit, nut, and citrus trees that need planting, weeding, harvesting, and feeding. There is watering, mowing, and pruning. There are seasonal schedules to be followed. A lot of research goes into this as I'm new to the gardeners' side of things.

The kitchen is where I spend a lot of my work hours. There are menus to look up and plan, shopping to keep pantries full, and inventory to manage. I have a strict budget and have found ways to make it stretch by planting my own organic food. I am also learning the craft of canning and drying food. Waste is down to almost nothing due to effective waste management by only buying what's needed, composting scraps, and either freezing, drying, or preserving what is near expiration. Most food is made from scratch so there are recipes to look up and new dishes to learn to cook all the time.

I am the house baker. There is no rising early to bake the loaves of the day. However, there is almost daily work required in the form of baking loaves of bread, crackers, and muffins. I make homemade tortillas. Some days there are even cakes to mix, rise, knead, and bake.

Then we have the finances. This one requires the writing up of budgets, strict buckling down, and using envelopes and restraint. Utilities and resources must be used wisely to keep the costs down. A savings must be built through cutting out excessive needs/wants and making do with what is at hand. Sometimes extensive research and investigation are needed to reduce interest rates on the house mortgage or new ideas incorporated such as solar panels and a clothesline. The bills must be paid in a timely manner and it is important that the funds are available at these times. Future retirement and education are also an investment to be worked toward so thrift and frugality are a must on all levels of running the home and tending to the family.

There are smaller jobs of baths for not just the children, but the dogs, as well. The trash bins must be taken out on garbage night.

Thought we were done? Oh no, Dear Reader, we have a bit to go yet. The duties of a House Manager are many.

There is the family wardrobe. This includes knowing everyone's sizes, searching in thrift stores, garage sales, and online at discount stores. It means accepting hand-me-downs with gratitude. There is the washing and organizing of all clothes. The storing of clothes that are not yet the right size or not for the season at hand. There are stains to wash out by hand, holes to be mended, and the occasional ironing. Though the washer kindly washes the clothes, at times, things need special washing in the sink or soaking in special solutions. In the warm seasons, clothes are hung outside on the garden clothesline. It is important that the family has the proper clothes for the weather, so inventory is key here. There is ordering the raincoats, snow boots, or whatever else is needed to keep everyone warm or well-ventilated.

Exercise is important. Children need park time, swimming time, nature hikes, and trips to the beach. The sun provides vitamin D, the fresh air cleans their lungs. My husband, Bali, does need some coaxing in this department at times, but it is important that the House Manager works out daily to keep her mood cheerful and her body strong for all the tasks and chores.

The house is to be made into a home and work is required to make it charming and cozy. This means more research in magazines, websites, and vlogs. Time and thought must be put into the decorating, and a small budget is to be adhered to. A small budget means many visits to browse the local hospice, thrift, or street yard sale for little treasures to fill the home with comfort and color.

Nutrition is important. Much studying and research must be done when it comes to illnesses, vaccines, organic food, and how to feed the family in a way that will reduce sickness, disease, and future doctor bills. This is where growing and preserving food comes in. Knowledge of vitamins and how to cook delicious and nutritious foods that everyone will eat and enjoy is crucial.

The pets also need care, healthy food, and veterinary appointments. Sometimes it's necessary to actually cook dog food from scratch or boil bone broth to ensure they stay healthy or recover from a mild doggy ailment.

Car maintenance, exercising the dogs, and heavy digging in the garden is left up to the mister of the house, along with working outside our humble abode to bring home the money I will then divide, save, and pay bills with.

Bali is the provider and protector. He is kind in doing all those small and large chores I set aside for him because the chores are either too strenuous, or have to do with cars, and that is far beyond my job knowledge.

I'm also the house nurse and counselor. You wouldn't think that a 5-year-old and a 7-year-old would need therapy, but those two are full of tiny world drama over stolen dinosaurs, a misplaced toy, or some little person insult that provokes wrath. I wipe many tears and have to mediate many arguments and help a little person navigate through feelings about life, the world, and others. I do this daily.

I have spent many nights up with sick ones and had to fuel myself with espressos to get through a 24-hour shift with little to no sleep. It comes with the territory.

I am also the house entertainment and activity director. I make sure we all have fun. I plan events to farms for apple picking during the fall, and I gather friends for Thanksgiving feasts. I plan a full month of Christmas celebrations that include baking, decorating, and singing carols. Outside of holidays, we have the seasonal crafts and celebrations. In the summer, we swim and hike. We take library trips weekly, play at the park, and meet friends for scheduled playdates. This doesn't happen all the time but it has to be planned and kept up. When I'm tired, I settle for reading books to the children, putting on music, and encouraging them to play on their own outside.

The last thing I can think of that is a major duty is the decluttering, organizing, and care of our household items. This requires going through cupboards, closets, and drawers often to keep things updated and clean. Keeping the clutter cleared helps in keeping an orderly house.

I believe that I've covered all my tasks. I'm not sure; I will probably think of a few more in the middle of the night but the point has been made.

Show your mother-in-law, sister, or neighbor this article when they suggest you go to "work" or get a "real job." Show this to your friend or spouse when they ask "What do you do all day?" Then, if it's a spouse, leave for the week on a family emergency (at the beach preferably) and let them figure out what to "do all day."

So, shall we begin this journey together?

I love this job more than anything. I am beyond grateful that I have the choice as some do not, and my heart goes out to them. I also take my job seriously. Oh sure, I joke about being lazy and letting the house go to pot, but the truth is that I clock in each morning while holding that homemade latte strong enough to peel the pretty paint on my walls, and I work *hard*. Some days are harder than others but by the end of the week and month I've built and scrubbed and planted and created a lot. Some days I'm planting my fall garden, other days I'm cleaning the whole house and rearranging the furniture to give it a fresh look, and then there are the days when the sink does fill up with dishes and the house looks disheveled because I worked on my writing all day. But lazy, I am not.

I am the matriarch of this house and I have earned the title and throne through labor and devotion. My family is my life and my home is my grown-up dollhouse to be loved, decorated, and played with. I have found great satisfaction in growing organic produce and learning the craft of canning and dehydrating food so as to not waste anything. I feel like I've gone back in time with my home because I practice so much of what I assume my grandmother and great-grandmother did daily.

Some books to help get you in the mood: *We Had Everything But Money* by Deb Mulvey, *The Complete Tightwad Gazette* by Amy Dacyczyn, and *Country Living* by Carla Emery.

Chapter 2

Working with a Small Budget

Ah, the small budget. This area is my specialty. I couldn't tell you what to do with piles of cash but I sure can help you live on a small, fixed income, single income, or any other type of restricted budget. I have done it many times when I was single and especially since getting married and starting a family.

When you are single, money can be a stressor if not handled properly. But when you have little babies to feed and provide shelter for, you just don't mess around. You get hardcore about having and sticking to a budget.

I became a homemaker and "retired" from the mainstream workforce right before having my first baby. During our first year as parents, Bali lost his job. I started a daycare but we lived in a small town where all the women had the same idea, so the competition was thick. Jobs were sparse. The only reason we didn't freak out was because we had some savings, enough to live on for almost a year. We had a roommate who helped out with rent, and I eventually received a family in my daycare that paid enough to take care of the bills, rent, as well as groceries to feed all of us, including the daycare children.

With this experience I learned to be industrious. I built my daycare from thrift stores and Craigslist. I used grocery envelopes and cooked everything at home. This was only the beginning.

We moved soon after to work for my husband's friend's brother (I know, a mouthful). Bali went from managing a large gas station and making a good living to cashiering in a dusty little river station for $10 per hour. We were grateful for the work despite the big changes.

You may wonder why the other job went under. Well, it was a thriving business, but a new boss took over, and gas and grocery deliveries rarely happened after that. What he was doing with the money is a guess, but a gas station doesn't thrive without groceries, beer, and cigarettes, and especially not without gas. I share this because you can think that all your ducks are in a row and then someone comes along or something unexpected happens and changes it all overnight. This was a gas station that should still be thriving to this day. This seaside town was a place I truly saw us growing old in. We had a lot of money coming in with the salary and a roommate. Life was cushy. However, one bad owner and it was all over with in a year.

A year later, we are living on a pear orchard near the Delta River and I'm reading *The Complete Tightwad Gazette* for the first time. It was at this point that I began reading the first of thousands of books, blogs, and articles on frugality that I would be digesting in rapid succession.

We had not made the big mistake most people make when they are living high on the hog. We did not buy a new car. We stuck with the car I brought into our marriage and for years, we only had the one car. We didn't obtain credit cards. We saved money when we were both working.

I had learned my lesson earlier in life and knew that cars, trinkets, eating out all the time, shopping, and opening credit cards leads to years upon years of working hard and stressing most nights until the piles of debt are paid off. This painful lesson would serve us the rest of our marriage.

Thus began my obsession and love for the simple and frugal life. I took it on as a challenge. I learned all I could, made tubs of laundry soap, hung our clothes on the old clotheslines out back, picked the fruit in season that surrounded our home, tried my hand at baking bread and sweets, and stuck to my grocery envelope and one day a week shopping trip with list and menus in hand.

When it came to my children, I nursed for a very long time, and I even tried my hand at cloth diapers. Unfortunately, they didn't have all the advice on YouTube they have now, and I couldn't find others who were using cloth diapers and could help me navigate the proper cleaning routine. When a bout of diarrhea took place, I was done. Today, I would stick with cloth and save that $40 to $80 a month.

I have come so far with what I do to save money. It is very fun, but it does take time to master and hone the skills. It's a new way of thinking and a very different lifestyle from most people. Anyone new to all of this: give yourself at least a year to adjust and make hundreds of wonderful mistakes.

I have a ringed notebook that I use for my budgeting. Every so often, I sit down with a calculator, pen, and highlighters and write out everything we pay for in a month. I then total up our earnings and subtract the outgoing from the incoming.

If more money is going out than coming in, I begin to cancel and cut whatever I can. Cable was something I cut out a long time ago. It's a silly line on the budget to have, with all the free and inexpensive things out there. I replaced cable with an antenna that Bali stuck on the roof for me, and now I enjoy local stations. We also purchased a cheap Smart TV and can watch YouTube, Netflix, and Vudu. Online, you can find Pluto, Tubi, Crackle, PBS, or pay for Hulu and Amazon Prime.

We live a very simple and inexpensive life and it may seem boring and uneventful to some but I don't feel like it is.

The boys and I wake up naturally almost every day unless we have an appointment. I make lovely, creamy, and sweet espresso lattes with my manual milk frother and stovetop Italian espresso maker. Then our day slowly unfolds for us.

It could be spent baking a batch of bread and working in the garden. It might be making a homemade pizza and cleaning the cottage. For the boys, it's playing and using their imaginations. I listen to all sorts of seminars on my laptop while I work. Studying and learning is something that feeds my soul. I learn about spiritual and mind matters, homesteading, and frugal living. I listen to authors talk about the craft of storytelling and writing books.

I spend my days learning recipes, fussing with my home, and enjoying my boys. This is not a sacrifice. This is a blessing.

But yes, we had to give up a lot of what most people find important to have what is truly meaningful to us in the end. **It is simply an exchange of one priority for another.**

It is up to you and your family to decide what is important but if more funds are leaving than coming in, it's time to assess things and downsize. It could be a huge downsize such as selling the 2,000 square foot house and purchasing a 1,200 square foot bungalow, or a simple downsize such as cutting out cable and finding more affordable cell phone plans.

Paying a small mortgage or rent is heaven and learning to reduce your utilities is rewarding. Every bit of money you save makes for a less stressful life.

Buying a fixer-upper in a neighborhood that is nice or on the up and up is a great way to find affordable housing in today's market. Make sure the home is solid and most of the work is cosmetic and things you and your partner can do by hand, such as painting or tearing out old carpet. If you feel confident in learning a little plumbing and electric, go for it. To save money, Bali and I have slowly become the Do-It-Yourself (DIY) couple.

What has become a bit popular is buying an old mobile home or a house on some land and remodeling it, planting gardens and raising animals.

To find a home that won't cost an arm and a leg will require thinking outside the box, being open and willing, and maybe some realistic evaluation of funds today, and into the future.

I know what it takes to have half the income go toward rent, and it really limits what you can do and save. When we decided to buy a house, my biggest desire was to pay less on the mortgage (including property tax and insurance) than we ever spent on rent. That was the only way it seemed worth it. We now pay less than $1,000 per month and this includes mortgage insurance protection, or MIP, because we didn't bring 20% down to the closing table. We pay $400 less per month on our mortgage payment than we ever did on rent since we've been married.

This summer we almost bought an old mobile home on 2 acres in the mountains. The home was solid and cozy but needed some fixing up and the land needed to be worked on. We were thrilled with the idea of painting and tilling like mad. It was very affordable and would have been even less than what we have now with the added bonus of land. I love nothing more than bringing an old house and property to life. Alas, it didn't work out this time.

If you aren't into gardening or yard upkeep, a small apartment or condominium could work out well and many are very cozy and attractive.

I would think about what you as a family or individual really need to be comfortable. In Europe and Asia, families live in teeny, tiny apartments, flats, and homes. It is only in America that we have to have the houses that are too large and each person has a bedroom. I think that children do better sharing a room. It encourages them to be together and bond instead of being in isolated rooms down the hall while on their laptops or cell phones. A smaller house brings a family together. It's true.

The next thing that will save you tons of money is paying off that financed car, or getting rid of it entirely, and buying a used car for cash. I can hear the arguments now, but you can get gently used cars in great shape, with low mileage, for a fabulous price. Both of our cars are used and have lasted for years without any problems. I paid one off quickly and we purchased the truck from a neighbor with cash. Not one regret. We have no car payments and the lower insurance is a phenomenal bonus.

I have heard of buying repossessed cars as well, you might look into that. There are ways to get good and new cars for cheap.

You could also consider getting rid of the cars altogether and bike or walk everywhere you can, and bus it or take a train to work. I lived without a car in the city for 10 years. Today we have the car and truck but the boys and I **walk** to parks, the library, post office, stores, farmers' market, and to visit their father at work.

Utilities

Getting solar power installed has been transformative when it comes to our electric bill. This summer many people have mentioned their $300 plus monthly bills. Ours is $87 for the solar and we pay $10 to Pacific Gas and Electric Company (PG&E) for hookup and another little amount around

$10 for natural gas. This summer, I ran the air conditioner quite a bit, and the bill did not increase.

We rent solar power through a company called V3 Electric. We have the option to buy at anytime but I like this better. We have free maintenance and repairs or replacements anytime without additional costs.

If you cannot purchase or rent solar power for whatever reason (e.g. they won't install it on a mobile unless you purchase it fully), then there are other ways I've found to cut the electric and gas bill.

The air conditioning units that go in the window are a huge savings as they don't require that much electricity and they crank out the cold air. I have a friend who has a small one in her little cabin and it cools the whole place to the point of it being *almost* too cold. One can be purchased at any of the big retailers: Walmart, Home Depot, Lowe's, www.amazon.com, etc. I am sure they can be found at many other places as well. The smaller ones run between $100 and $200 and are so worth it.

The Presto Heat Dish is a plug in heater I was introduced to last winter, and I used it solely for most of the milder part of winter. It keeps a small room warm, and my electric bill didn't seem to be affected at all. This is shocking as plug in heaters can put you in debt quickly. I would only encourage the use of this specific heater. I've used others and almost fainted when I received the electric bill. I tried this heater out for a few months prior to our solar power being turned on, so I'm pretty confident that this is true.

In older houses, the insulation tends to be sparse or non-existent and the windows may be of the single pane variety. Thick, insulating curtains will keep the heat in. Carpet on the floor helps as well, and if you have wood floors, be sure to invest in huge area and hall rugs for the winter. I purchased thick, long curtains at Big Lots one year when we had the thin windows and was amazed at how well it kept that chill out, and the warmth in. Last winter, I spread large rugs in every room and down the hall and it made a noticeable difference. The rugs were purchased at nice thrift stores or on sale on www.amazon.com.

I have many other little tricks I use to keep the costs down. We haven't had our solar very long, but for years, we suffered the increasing PG&E bills. I never have lights on during the day and use only lamps at night in whatever room we are in. No one in this house leaves the lights on; we are all well-trained. It helps to unplug as well since power is still surging through wires when plugged in, even if the appliance is off. TVs are on only when in use. Most of my appliances are the Energy Saver type.

If you have a wood stove, see if you can find local orchards and ask if you could haul away the dead trees when they clear out the old parts of an orchard. This is how we used to get enough free wood for many winters when we lived out on the farm.

When we first moved in to this old house we did the Weatherization Assistance Program with PG&E. They will seal windows and doors, insulate your attic, change out every light bulb with LED (this alone was worth over $300), replace shower heads for water saving, and get you a microwave if you don't have one, as they consider that to be an energy saver. They may even replace an old appliance. It is definitely worth looking into and even if you rent you can get the landlord's permission and proceed.

There are programs for roof replacement and solar power installation when you are low income and dealing with an old house. Check in your state and county to see what programs you may qualify for.

Now, let's talk water. We are in Northern California and with our mediterranean climate and bouts of drought, we are careful. Having two kitchen gardens that take up what was once a lawn, and something like 23 fruit, citrus, and nut trees makes this tricky. Let's not forget our grapevines. Surprisingly, we only went over our flat rate once and it was a mere $1.10 extra. The flat rate is for sewage and water.

Mulch was a huge water saver. We found people giving away mulch in a nearby city. There are programs that will connect you with a tree service company and when they have wood chips from a day's work they will come to your house and dump their truck load instead of taking it to the dump. The only problem is that it's a huge truck and much more than most of us need with our suburban backyards. People get too much mulch and then advertise it on Craigslist to get the enormous pile out of their driveway. This is where we come along and take a truck load off their hands. We scored two piled high loads this summer after being inspired by the documentary, *Back to Eden*.

Mulch changes your soil for the better, making it

richer and more drainable. It helps it to hold in water. We spread it on all the gardens, trees, and even in our containers of flowers and herbs. Once the garden plants are well-established, I only water once a week, even in triple digit heat. The trick is to water deeply and well. If the plants are getting wilty I will water a bit more but it wasn't necessary this year. God bless that mulch!

You can use graywater but be careful what laundry soap you use. It's easy to move the back hose from the washer into a rain barrel to get all the water and then use on the lawn or trees and flowers. It isn't recommended to use on food plants or fruit trees. I have some people tell me it is just fine, and others say not to. It's worth a look. Eco-friendly laundry detergent is safe for graywater.

If you don't want to mess with hoses on the washer then you can use bath water, shower water, and dish water. Once again, be careful with soaps. You don't want salts to build up. Dr. Bronner's castile soap is safe and most bar soaps and shampoos are mild enough. We use the boys' bath water on the lawn and when I run water in the shower or sink to get it hot, I have a bucket catching the water. I then use this clean water for container plants and fruit trees. We even go so far as to dump an old glass of drinking water in a plant instead of down the sink and we never just run the water while brushing our teeth. Like I said, it all adds up because we never go over the flat rate (except for that one time) and we have a fruit and vegetable farm.

As for phones and TV, that is up to you. There are antennas and free sites for TV programs and movies, as previously mentioned and listed. We have family all over the United Kingdom, India, and Canada, so we have our phone service with Vonage, a Voice over Internet Protocol company (VoIP), and we can call everyone for only $29 a month. Our cell phone service plans are $25 per month for each line with MetroPCS (no contract, which I love, in case I find a better plan with a different company). I wouldn't even have a cell phone but I travel with the boys and it's a great thing to have in an emergency situation. I also use it a lot to record my YouTube videos and take photos for my blog and my boys (because they are so yummy).

Other than that, we don't have much else except insurance policies. We have homeowners insurance, basic car insurance, medical insurance for the family through a plan called Covered California, and a small life insurance policy. I have thought about pet insurance after taking my sweet cat to the animal emergency hospital and then having to put her down, but I am still pondering that.

I don't tithe, as I don't have a church that I attend. I do set aside around $100 each month for donating to large and reputable non-profit organizations. Be very careful in donating to a program and make sure they are well-known and respected. Many charities will beg for money and you have no idea where it is really going.

Mary Hunt, a frugal living author, suggests that you live on 80% of your income, save 10%, and donate the other 10%.

Here is Mary Hunt's blog for great money saving tips: https://www.everydaycheapskate.com/

Mary Hunt put her family $100,000 in debt in 12 years and spent the next 13 paying back every penny. She worked 3 jobs, including odd jobs. She even ironed other people's laundry, and learned everything she could to save money and cut costs. If anyone knows how to save money and be frugal, it is this woman.

I have followed many wise frugalistas to save and reduce. Even the smallest and most silly sounding tips will save at least a few dollars a year. It adds up to thousands before you know it.

How To Save $1,000 Monthly

We do not follow Mary's 80-10-10 suggestion at this time. We have a very large goal in mind that will bring us a lot of joy, comfort, and security in the future. I made a goal of saving $1,000 a month to reach this goal as fast as possible. To do this we skim the first $1,000 of the top at the beginning of the month. That means that the very first paycheck of the month goes right into our savings account. As I have mentioned in my YouTube videos and previous books, the savings account is in a separate bank and is never touched or even looked at. We deposit the money and step away quickly.

The next paycheck goes to the mortgage, which is paid 2 weeks early at that point. Then, we receive some royalties and affiliate program payments. The amounts vary from month to month, but it's always enough to cover the utilities, donations, gas for the vehicles, and groceries. Some royalty payments are more lean and require creativity, such as more walking and less driving trips, searching out coupons and deals at the grocery store, and eating beans and rice more often than we may enjoy.

I set aside and pay approximately $85 per month in donations. Not much, but as our income increases or more cash is freed up, I increase my donations. I'd rather stay small for the time being so that I can always give instead of donating too much and when finances are tight, having to quit. That has happened before when we had some financial issues. It felt depressing. Start out small with the giving and increase the sharing as your abundance grows.

I try to give us a certain amount for gas but as you know, the prices increase and decrease constantly. During the school year, I drive up into the mountains for two different school programs for the boys. Sure, if we needed to give that up, we would, and could make do at home, but these programs bring so much joy to my boys and they thrive in them both so it's worth the driving and extra gas.

Food, Glorious Food!

We love cooking and enjoying delicious meals and snacks. You might say that we are a bit food driven at times when the aromas are wafting through our home. It seems that nothing is as marvelous as the moment we all look forward to: sitting down to enjoy a hot, homemade meal.

The boys are growing as are their appetites. I'm big on clean and wholesome foods and try to buy as much organic food as possible. This combo gets expensive.

The USDA has a food plan chart that I like to use:

https://fns-prod.azureedge.net/sites/default/files/media/file/CostofFoodAug2019.pdf

I found this chart to be very enlightening and comforting. I used to watch YouTube videos where the family would only spend small amounts on groceries each month and I felt like a failure if I couldn't get my budget as low. What was I doing wrong?

Well, here is part of the secret: most of those people already have stocked pantries, freezers, and cupboards. It's easy to keep the tab low when you are just getting odds and ends to add to what you already have. Some people grow food, raise animals, milk goats, and have eggs from their hens.

Some people dumpster dive or go to food pantries at the end of the day to glean what will be thrown away.

There are many ways to save on groceries and it doesn't have to include coupon clipping. You could certainly do that and there are websites that will guide you and send you emails to help you collect coupons. One site that is fun and helpful is The Krazy Coupon Lady: https://thekrazycouponlady.com/

I have gone to large farms that have U-Pick programs. At one of our nearest farms, I can pick my own produce for 30 cents a pound, but the catch is that you must pick no less than 100 pounds. This is fantastic for canning and $30 for 100 pounds of produce is an amazing deal.

Some farms will let you glean what is left in the field after the harvest. Some orchards have U-Pick programs for apples and other fruit, as well.

Other programs include community-supported agriculture (CSA) box deliveries of local produce and sometimes meat, dairy, and eggs. You can even see about volunteering in exchange for a box.

I have found that the best way is to learn to grow my own food. It takes some labor in the beginning, but as the years go by, you begin harvesting more and more. It is delicious, fresh, organic food that only cost a few dollars in seeds plus labor. Each year, the work is less, easier, and you can save seeds for future planting to reduce the cost as well.

As for shopping budgets, I have played with my grocery budget for years and this is the least expensive and healthiest way to do it, hands down (for us, at least).

First off, you **get real** about what you can put aside for groceries and you put it into a cash envelope. This helps you stick to the allotted amount. When that envelope is empty, you are done. In the beginning it's tricky and sometimes stressful as you may spend it all in the first two weeks, and then panic about the next two weeks. The end of the month can consist of a very bland diet as you stretch out those potatoes and frozen peas. Ah, but you will become a master creator after a couple of these months, believe me.

Only buy produce that is in season. Seasonal fruits and vegetables taste far better and travel far less. Try to eat locally grown food. It supports and encourages local farms. The food is fresher and of a higher quality.

Buy in bulk and in large quantities. I am a co-op member with our health food store and I buy organic flour, wheat, grains, oats, beans, and lentils in 25 lb to 50 lb bags to save money. I also have a fully stocked pantry. Educate yourself on how to best store this bulk food and how long it will keep. For example, wheat doesn't keep very long; it goes rancid in about 2 months. Sugar lasts for 30 years (of course).

Store your bulk items in airtight buckets. These can be found at WinCo Foods, Home Depot, and sometimes at various health food stores and hardware stores. Some things should be frozen to kill bugs. It may be gross, but organic foods are alive and attract live things; be thankful for that. Not even a bug will touch chemical-laden food and we should think about that before we fill our bellies with grains drenched in Roundup.

A good documentary to help you decide whether organics are worth it, or if you are on the fence about it, is *Secret Ingredients*. You can find it on YouTube as well as their website: https://secretingredientsmovie.com/

Buy a huge bag of flour and wheat. Some of you who are gluten intolerant can't do this but those of you who aren't, do invest in a large bag of flour and learn the craft of baking and mixing. You can make your own sourdough, wheat bread, Amish white bread, pancakes, muffins of all kinds, restaurant-style breadsticks, pizza dough, cakes, cookies, bars, and much, much more. Turn your house into a bakery. For those of you who are on gluten-free diets, I'm sure there are other great flours out there such as almond flour and oat flour.

Go vegetarian! Or just cut way back on the animal products. I used to buy a whole chicken and bake that for the week. I found that sectioning it up after baking and using it in whole dishes such as casseroles, enchiladas, soups, and salads would stretch it out significantly. We really don't need that much protein. Let's think about the typical diet in the early 1900s. Meat was a luxury and used sparingly. Sunday was the only time a full roast or chicken would be served along with a pie, cake, or other dessert. Sugar and meat were special food items, not served at each meal as they are now.

When my family and I are in our carnivorous stage (we have bouts of this, followed by stretches of plant-based eating without animal products), our total consumption is typically four whole chickens, a pound of ground beef, and two pounds of an inexpensive fish such as red snapper. This is for the **whole month**. I find that when we cut out all animal products we feel better and the bill is smaller. However, there are times we crave it and I will cook it because I am a firm believer in listening to the body's signals. I think that children should be eating a great variety of foods and never be restricted, as they need so much to grow and thrive (except when they say they are craving cake).

Less cow. If you love cream in your coffee, switching to milk might be less expensive and contain less calories and fat. We drink icy cold, fresh water all the time. Milk isn't as good for you or children as the dairy council would have you believe. You can make your own nut or hemp seed milks and use coconut butter to cook or bake with. It's better for you and may save some money.

Water, lots of water. Cold water is what we are used to so we love it. I love mine with ice, or sometimes we spruce it up with a little cranberry juice or lemon juice and Stevia. Soda is a special occasion type of drink. Milk is never had. I do give my children goat milk as a treat now and then or some nut, oat, or hemp milk with a peanut butter and jelly sandwich. But water is the main household beverage. Try adding mint leaves, cucumber slices, or even melon chunks in a pitcher of water and keep in the fridge.

Recently, I had some health issues. Fortunately, I have friends that are ER nurses who are also into a more holistic approach to healing. It turned out that I was dehydrated. I said this was impossible since I drink so much water throughout the day. But when we just drink plain water, we wash out electrolytes. If you are very active or out in the heat, sweating, you need to replace the electrolytes.

Here is a recipe for poor man's electrolytes: a quart of water, a few ounces of orange or lemon juice and a pinch of sea salt. I truly felt great after doing this and continue to do a quart a day and then plain water the rest of the day.

Cook from scratch. The more you cook and prepare meals from scratch, the more money you save. I have found that when I don't buy any packaged food at all, my grocery bill is half of what it is if I'm purchasing that frozen Stouffer's lasagna, the bags of chips, the premade sauces and rice, and the cake mixes. However, there are times when that box of macaroni and cheese or that .99 boxed cake will save you time and money. Overall, however, scratch cooking is the way to go.

Quit the harmful habits. We do not drink alcohol and that saves hundreds of dollars a month, truly. I know people who cry, "poor" and I can't help but think that cutting out the good beers and fine wines each month would free up a couple hundred dollars for groceries or bills. We don't use any other recreational drugs, either, such as marijuana or pills. This saves even more money for bills, food, and fun. I bring this up because I have observed others who live a very poor lifestyle. They constantly struggle with the ability to pay their bills for basic needs such as water and electricity. They never have enough to buy the monthly groceries. They somehow always have money for cigarettes, however. I would feel compassion for them, but I see the daily pot smoking and almost nightly drinking. I know from past experience that all these things cost a lot of money even if you are drinking the cheap discount beers and $2 boxed wines. Cigarettes cost some crazy amount, like $8 a pack! This is money that could stock the pantries with rice, beans, eggs, and apples. This is money that could cover the electric and water bill easily.

Addictions are very hard to quit but so, *so* worth it in the end; and not just in saving thousands of dollars that could be spent to provide a higher quality of life, but improving one's mental and physical health and well-being. It's what I'd call *priceless*.

Jump start frugality and start a savings account. Here is the secret formula to completely turn your financial situation around and begin a new lifestyle (only if you want). This is the stripped down, quick version. I put this at the end for those of you that need to do a big overhaul. You can start here and then go back and add the extra little ways to cut costs.

Here it goes:

First, you and your spouse or partner get out a good old-fashioned, 3-ring binder, pencils, and a calculator. It's a good idea to pull up your accounts online, as well.

Write your monthly income on the top of the page. Next, you list everything you pay for monthly: rent/mortgage, utilities, insurance premiums, cars, cable, phones, Internet and on and on.

Then, you figure out all the gas you use in the cars monthly. If you also have bus, train or commuter tickets, add those.

Last, but most important because this is where you will more than likely be shocked, but will also be able to make huge and fast changes: add groceries and all food! But this is every single time you make a trip to the store, the mini mart, the snacks at the gas station, the cafe, Starbucks, going out to eat, breakfast out on weekends, dinners out, takeout, pizza deliveries, and Chinese food. Every stick of gum!

For this, you may need to look at your bank

statements or take a notepad and follow yourselves around for a month uncensored. Write down every soda, bottled water, meal, bite, and sip you pay for outside the home and every time you forget something like "milk" or "that mix" at the store. Those times you go to only get those items and come back with five bags of groceries.

You may choke a bit or want to faint. But the exciting part is that this is where you will see a fast change.

Now, add up everything and subtract from the monthly income. Are you over or under?

If under, then fabulous. Find a way to save that extra money.

Over? Drat. Well, here is the fix-it-fast program. You may want to brew up a pot of coffee and read this over and then meditate on it. If you are over, then you're probably covering costs with credit cards and digging a hole of debt and feeling the stress in those quiet hours.
First, get into all the wallets (yours and partner's) and cut up all the credit cards. You do NOT need credit cards for credit. This is a lie and you have been brainwashed. I was told years ago that I need so many credit cards to prove good credit. What hogwash. I then spent six years working three jobs to pay off all that marvelous "credit."

Before Bali and I purchased our first house we had to fix our credit. Bali had bad credit and I had none because after I paid off my debt I paid in cash for everything for years. I had zero credit.

We both obtained **secured credit cards** through

our bank with a balance of $300 each. It is simply a small savings account with a faux credit card. A credit card with training wheels, if you will. You open an account with $300 of your own money and they give you this pretend credit card, and each month you buy all your groceries and gas on it, and then fill it up. That is it. Spend it all and fill it up completely each month. Bali and I had over 700 point credit scores within a year. I believe 850 is the highest you can go according to some sources. Be sure to check your bank's terms and conditions for secured credit cards in order to avoid any penalties or fees they may have.

Another bit of advice is to **not** call the credit card companies to cancel. Just cut them up and start paying them off using Dave Ramsey's snowball method. Look it up on Google. He has a book titled, *The Complete Money Makeover.* He also has a podcast, lots of workshops, more books, and more. He has some great advice and is well-respected. I do some things differently but have taken on many of his suggestions. I actually just ordered his book from the library for the third time, as we want to pay off our mortgage quickly.

Okay, so you did the budget, cut up the credit cards, ordered Dave Ramsey's book from the library, went into your bank, and signed up for secured credit cards. Now what?

You stop spending. Period. You do one of those popular "no spend" months. How you do that is you pay the rent/mortgage, utilities, cell phone bills, commuting costs, and that is it. No eating out, shopping, Target runs, roaming about Walmart, or the mall. Not even a stick of gum at the gas station.

But what about food, crazy Kate?! You go through those cluttered pantries, cupboards, freezer, and fridge that are probably packed from the constant shopping and you make out a month of menus. You may need to clean and organize said pantries and fridge to get rid of expired things and take proper inventory. Some of us had jobs in retail stores and we know what it is like to take inventory. You have to get rid of expired foods (some may be fine, still), and organize foods in categories such as pasta, beans, sauces, mixes, and so on. You then see if you have enough and can be creative enough to make 30 days' worth of meals. Here is where you may need to do one big shopping trip. But only one, so do this carefully, listing everything you will need to round out the meals. Stock up on coffee and tea for you shan't be frequenting any coffee house.

That first month is grueling because you will be overcoming addictions you had no idea were present within your soul. You will want to go to the grocery store just to get the heck out of the house. You will want to go to Dollar Tree to see what new items they may have. You will want someone else to make your latte...

If you can power through this month you will save hundreds, maybe even a thousand or more dollars just from staying home and cooking at home. You will begin to break the addiction of shopping and going out. It's just a way to stay busy and avoid. Avoid what? I don't know, that is between you and you. You will find a creative side you never knew existed. You will even begin to enjoy being home.

Start making money while you do a no spend

month. Take this month of being home and get busy in other, more productive and lucrative ways. Start decluttering on a mass level. If you have a full garage or even a storage unit, it's time to clear them out and organize. Keep what you will use right now in your house or yard and start cleaning out everything else.

Why not? You won't be going out for four weekends; believe me, you will need an extracurricular activity.

Start selling things on eBay and Craigslist. Have big, fat garage sales every weekend. How fun! Getting rid of clutter and making money. It's addictive. At first it's hard to do but it gets easier and you get more organized and can whip it together faster. Be sure to advertise!

Educate yourself during this no-spend hiatus. This is a great time to learn all you can about saving money, being thrifty and frugal, and cutting costs. Use YouTube and Google for information on saving on electricity and water, cutting down on groceries and any and all bills. I have found great channels to inspire wise ways to shop and garden, reduce waste, and thrift.

Pro Home Cooks is a YouTube channel with an assortment of things that may not interest you but it has many old vlogs on there from a previous channel called *Brothers Green Eats*. The brothers split but this channel has the old videos about how to buy healthy groceries for a week for the amount of what you would spend on a latte a day or all the healthy food you could prepare for the amount you would spend on a Domino's pizza.

Here are a couple of links to check out:

https://www.youtube.com/watch?v=NyyJqX30-NA&t=27s This is what you can cook for the price of a Domino's pizza. It's amazing!

https://www.youtube.com/watch?v=zjeY6Bzg6jw This one shows you what you can eat for the price of a coffee a day. You will not believe it.

https://www.youtube.com/watch?v=B4TfxcPzZEs For those of you going hardcore, this video is about living on $0 a day!

Go on my YouTube channel, *Coffee With Kate* and look at the channels I subscribe to. There, you can find a great variety of channels that include cooking, gardening, budgeting, homesteading, and so much more. I also have a playlist to find specifics under "Cooking," "Spiritual," and "Budget."

Chapter 3

Building a Grocery Store and Cafe in Your Kitchen

Your pantry will become your personalized grocery store. You will no longer need to run around like a wild hen trying to gather items from multiple stores. With a steaming coffee mug in your hand, you will calmly walk over to your pantry or pantry area and browse your inventory.

I built up quite the pantry when I started to truly cook from scratch and veganize all of our foods. We are not vegan, but we love to eat mostly plant-based. I actually love most vegan foods over their animal counterparts now. It was when I was trying to convert a meat or dairy dish to a vegan dish that required more spices and herbs that I truly began to learn the craft of scratch cooking and baking.

I knew I had become a professional housewife when I would think up a menu, say a casserole and chocolate cake for a Sunday supper, and I had all the necessary ingredients right there in the comfort of my home. How fun! I turned on my $2 thrift store radio and listened to a local station that plays mostly 70s and 80s hits (my favorite for doing kitchen work) and I stirred, simmered, chopped, mixed, and frosted my way to a fantastic meal to serve my family. And I never left the house.

Then I got into making my own cleaners and laundry soaps and began stockpiling Zote brand soap, washing soda, huge jugs of white vinegar, and Borax. I would run out of something and just pull some boxes and bottles from the shelf and mix in a spray bottle and voila! Other times I would boil up a tub of laundry soap for the year.

Now, let's talk about how to build your pantry so that you can make a casserole, cake, laundry soap, even shampoo or some playdough for the kids without ever leaving your home.

First off, find a space. Some of you have pantries. Some of us had to create them. I converted my water heater closet and laundry room. Some laundry rooms will be too damp and warm so think about it carefully. Mine is very airy and dry as it is off the kitchen and bedroom and has the back door as well as a window that keeps it dry. I already had some large kitchen shelving and utilized those to make said pantry. I also have a lot of shelves in my kitchen and could make even more room in the cupboards if the need arises.

You can convert a shoe closet, put bins under your bed, use shelves in the closet, and/or put shelving in the garage and create a huge pantry in there. Be creative.

For stockpiling and building a pantry you can use coupons, stock up on sale items, and even can and preserve your own foods.

To know what to stockpile you would sit down with the big notebook that you used to do your budget and write down all your cleaning and washing products on one page and all the things your family eats and drinks on another page. Get an idea of what you cook and fix daily, weekly, and monthly. Don't forget holidays and birthdays; you need cake mixes and such.

I have both a cleaning pantry and a food pantry. The food pantry holds many canned and dried goods. I bulk shop and have shelves filled with jars of things to aid in scratch cooking. I buy 25 lbs to 50 lbs of organic flours, grains, legumes, and oats that I store in 5-gallon airtight buckets.

There are many fun and helpful books that you may enjoy. These are just a few:

Dining on a Dime by Tawra Kellam and Jill Cooper
Dump Dinners by Cathy Mitchell
Dump Desserts by Cathy Mitchell
Make-A-Mix Cookery by Karine Eliason, Nevada Harward, and Madeline Westover
The New Farm Vegetarian Cookbook (Vegan) by Louise Hagler
The Joy of Cooking by Irma Rombauer, Marion Rombauer Becker, and Ethan Becker

These books will teach you how to make every single mix you can imagine. You will never need another boxed or packaged mix again. They will also help you build your pantry and make cooking from scratch easy. I'm not crazy about every recipe in these books but I've learned so much and had so much fun working with all of them. The more I cook from scratch, the more our grocery bill shrinks, and I believe our waistlines do, too. It also helps me to keep the chemicals, dyes, and junk out of my family's diet.

Below, I have a basic pantry list to get you started. It may sound boring but I will break down just what can be made from each item. When you get deep into making everything at home, from the beginning to the end, you will know that a sack of flour is not just a sack of flour. It is a bakery waiting to unfold.

Starters For Your New Pantry (Super Cheap & Basic)

One way to save a huge amount of your monthly income is to learn to shop and cook differently. I recently uploaded a vlog about jumpstarting frugality. It is about extreme ways to start living below your means. This topic goes with it perfectly.

I love working from cookbooks that help you build your pantry and show you how to make everything under the sun using simple ingredients. I have found that *Dining On A Dime*, *Make-A-Mix Cookery*, *Dump Dinners*, and *Dump Desserts* (all referenced above) do exactly that.

After reading and working from these books, I have made a list of absolute must-haves to stock a proper pantry that will provide you with all the basics for scratch cooking.

- 25 lbs to 50 lbs of all-purpose flour
- 25 lbs of wheat flour
- 50 lbs of pinto beans
- 25 lbs of rice (white or brown)
- 20 bags of assorted pasta (spaghetti, macaroni, egg noodles, bow tie, etc.)
- 50 lbs of potatoes (russets are the cheapest)
- 20 lbs of onions (we prefer red)

- Large box or bag of powdered milk
- 20 large bags of frozen and mixed vegetables
- 25 lb bag of oats
- Huge jars of peanut butter
- 10 cans of water-packed tuna
- 10 lb bag of sugar
- 8 large cans of tomato sauce
- 1 to 2 lbs of raisins
- 20 lb bag of coffee (of course)
- A large container of powdered creamer

Seasonings (I purchase most of my seasonings from the bulk section at WinCo Foods):

- A gallon of oil (a healthy one, preferably)
- 2 or more lbs of salt
- 1/2 lb of granulated onion (I prefer the flavor much more than the powdered)
- 1/2 lb of granulated garlic
- 1/2 cup of Italian seasoning
- 1/2 cup dried thyme
- 1/2 cup dried basil
- 1/2 cup dried parsley
- 1/2 cup dried rosemary

Extra bulk seasonings to make dishes from scratch:

- 1 lb or more of cheese powder mix
- 1 lb of powdered peanut butter
- 1/2 cup chicken flavor powder

With these foods, you can make all your own crackers, cakes, bread, tortillas, fried potatoes and onions, mashed potatoes, casseroles, macaroni and cheese, bean dishes, burritos, soups, hot cereals, and more.

This is just a big and quick pantry starter list, but if you add to it each month with extra money from your grocery envelope, you will have nutritious and filling meals that taste delicious and down-home.

Once you have the basics, you can start adding:

- Big bags of corn tortillas for homemade chips and tacos.
- Large boxes of Krusteaz cornbread and pancake mixes. I love these as they only require water, and at the end of the month, you don't always have the oil, eggs, or milk that other mixes call for.
- Canned chili, beans (kidney, pinto, black, cannellini, garbanzo) and vegetables (all purchased on sale).
- Anything that your family likes, is on sale, and can be added to stretch a meal.

- Popcorn (don't forget that!)

Produce:

- Bananas (always very inexpensive)
- Any produce in season
- Large bags of carrots
- Celery
- Fruits and vegetables packaged in large bags as opposed to loose. For example, loose oranges will usually cost more than a 10 lb bag of oranges.

Condiments:

- Pickles
- Mayonnaise
- Mustard
- Ketchup

Some people go to food banks at the end of the day or month to ask for what they are about to throw out. This way, you are not taking from anyone in need, but saving food from the garbage. You can preserve and dehydrate the food quickly before it truly spoils.

If you need to save money, learn to live on less than

you earn. If you are in debt, it is an absolute must to pay it off as quickly as possible. You can use your creative powers and become very industrious about foraging food, both inside and out of the city or town that you live in.

But always, always have fun! Make it into a game and learn the craft.

Kitchen Equipment

You don't need a lot of fancy gadgets and gizmos. These are the items with which I have gotten by just fine. If you don't have an item, check your local thrift stores. I just purchased a new George Foreman Lean Mean Fat Reducing Grill at the thrift store for $8 and a food processor at the Grange Co-op for $39.

- Iron skillets
- Wok with lid (optional)
- Funnel (optional, but helpful in many situations)
- Metal spatula
- Ladle
- Wooden spoons
- Hand mixer
- Juicer (an inexpensive brand like Hamilton Beach works great)
- Food processor
- Blender (this should be a good one; you'll be making oat flour and green smoothies with it)
- Hand grater (not super necessary with the food processor in competition)
- Pots with lids
- Large slow cooker

- Rice cooker
- Colander
- Stovetop Italian espresso maker
- Stovetop percolator (optional)
- Tea kettle

Bulk Cooking

You don't have to sweat over a hot stove all day. You can have a day of just baking for the week. How about shopping early in the morning one day and prepping food for the week the following day?

I do this sometimes. I'll bake a chicken, cook a huge pot of beans, steam a big pot of rice, bake a few loaves of bread, and make a batch of tortilla dough. These dishes can be mixed and matched to make burritos and casseroles. You can also just serve a big plate of rice, beans, a little chicken, and tortillas on the side.

I'm very much into easy, quick, affordable cooking that is also delicious. We love a tasty, hot meal, and it has to be loaded with lots of nutrients so that we feed our little boys properly in order for them to grow and thrive, and the husband and I stay strong and healthy.

I use my big, cast iron skillet and big pots for everything. I only cook one big meal a day and we eat supper at an earlier time than most, between 2:00 p.m. and 3:00 p.m. But I cook a ton of food so if anyone is hungry later, they can help themselves. There is usually enough to pack Bali's lunch the next day as well as leftovers for more meals.

Chapter 4

Kate's Staple Dishes & Family Favorites

I will be sharing many recipes and meal ideas throughout this book. You will find that some do not have any measurements provided. Please be advised that these are a method, as I don't use exact measurements when whipping them up. You can add your favorite ingredients and switch them up to make them your own. Experiment and have fun in your kitchen!

You can check out my channel and get a glimpse of my cooking. It's not fancy whatsoever, but it is filling, delicious, and healthy. Here are some dishes that I like to make:

Slow Cooker Potatoes

Wash a bag of potatoes and fill up your large slow cooker, as many as will comfortably fit inside.

Cook on high heat for 4 to 6 hours.

Just poke a potato with a fork to see if it is soft. I store them in the refrigerator once they cool. You can reheat them for days as baked and loaded potatoes or turn them into fried potatoes and onions.

Beans

Beans are a great money saver. They are full of protein, complex carbohydrates, and fiber, and are very easy to cook!

Just sort beans (at least a pound, in order to have plenty for the week), remove any debris or rocks, wash well in plenty of water, and drain.

Place them into a large pot with water. Make sure the water is a few inches above the beans and simmer for several hours on low to medium heat.

Keep checking and adding water as they triple in size and suck up all the water.

Add sea salt to taste, or whatever salt you prefer or have on hand.

They taste best the next day after sitting in the refrigerator all night and then being reheated. Some dishes improve with time and make the best leftovers. Beans freeze excellently, as well.

Potatoes & Onions

Preheat pan and add a couple of tablespoons of oil.

Slice an onion and saute for a couple of minutes.

 Add chopped, pre-cooked potatoes and let them get brown and a bit crispy.

Serve with pinto beans.

You can add whatever toppings or condiments you'd

like. Sour cream and hot sauce are wonderful. I like to use ketchup on my fried potatoes.

Macaroni & Cheese with Vegetables

This is another easy dinner!

Make macaroni and cheese according to package directions.

In a separate pan, add some oil, sliced red onions, and saute for a bit.

Add a big bag of any frozen vegetables you like.

I love the mixed kind that has peas, corn, carrots, and green beans.

Saute for a long time, until the vegetables are fully warmed through and soft.

Then, add a little bit of butter, salt, and pepper to taste.

Serve with macaroni and cheese. So good!

Corn Bread

I take a huge box of Krusteaz corn bread and make a big cake pan of it.

This can be served for a couple of days with a side salad, green beans or other vegetables. It goes perfectly with a bowl of home-cooked beans or chili, as well.

Here is a collection of family favorite recipes that I've been making over the years:

Peasant Bread

Ingredients

3 cups warm water

2 Tbsp yeast

5 cups white flour (you can substitute a cup for bran or flax)

2 or more cups wheat flour

Directions

In a large bowl, add 3 cups warm water (not *too* warm or it will kill the yeast) and sprinkle yeast in.

Add 5 cups white flour or 3 to 4 cups and 1 to 2 cups flax, bran, or whatever sounds good to you.

Stir, cover with a damp cloth, and let sit and rise for 1 hour.

Once risen, add the additional 2 cups of wheat flour and stir.

Pour onto a floured surface and knead it until it is no longer sticky. You may have to add more flour as you go.

Put back in the bowl and cover with the damp cloth. Let rise for another hour.

After the second rise, punch down and divide in half. Place each half into bread pans. Cover again for a third rise.

Bake in the oven at 350 degrees Fahrenheit for 35 to 50 minutes.

This recipe is very adaptable. You can add anything to change it. Some examples: nuts, dried raisins and cinnamon, butter and honey (that is what the original recipe calls for), or make it super healthy with all sorts of oat bran and wheat bran.

Amish White Bread (source: www.allrecipes.com)

Ingredients

2 cups warm water

2/3 cups sugar

1 ½ Tbsp active dry yeast

1 ½ tsp salt

¼ cup oil

6 cups white flour

Directions

In a large bowl, mix water and yeast and let sit for about 5 minutes.

Add sugar, oil, salt, and flour last.

Mix and pour out onto floured surface and knead until no longer sticky (may need to add more flour).

Return to bowl and cover with damp cloth and let rise for 1 hour.

Once risen, punch down and divide in half.

Make into loaves and put into pans.

Cover with damp cloth again and let rise once more.

Bake at 350 degrees Fahrenheit for 30 to 40 minutes.

Tortillas (source: www.tasteofhome.com)

Ingredients

2 cups white flour (you can use half wheat, if you'd like)

½ teaspoon salt

¾ cup water

3 Tbsp oil

Directions

In a large bowl, add all ingredients.

Mix and knead, adding more flour or water if necessary. Let sit for 20 minutes.

Make into small balls and roll out onto a floured surface.

In a large skillet, cook tortillas over medium heat for approximately 1 minute on each side, or until lightly brown.

Keep and serve warm.

Mushroom Stroganoff (source: *Simply Sara Kitchen* on YouTube)

Ingredients

1 lb button mushrooms, sliced (or any kind you prefer or whatever's on sale)

1 onion, diced

2 Tbsp olive oil

2 Tbsp butter

4 cloves minced garlic

1 Tbsp Worcestershire sauce

4 Tbsp white flour

3 cups vegetable stock

½ cup sour cream

¼ tsp thyme

Salt to taste

Granulated or powdered garlic to taste

Granulated or powdered onion to taste

Black pepper to taste

Directions

Saute mushrooms and diced onions in the butter and oil until all the liquid from the mushrooms has cooked down/evaporated.

Add garlic and Worcestershire sauce and saute for about a minute.

Sprinkle in the white flour, cook, and stir a couple more minutes.

Add vegetable stock, stir.

Add all seasonings: salt, garlic powder, onion powder, pepper, and thyme.

Simmer on low heat and add sour cream.

This is so delicious over egg noodles. I eat too many helpings. Sometimes I double the batch, we love it so much. Hands down, this recipe is one of my favorites!

Spaghetti with French Bread

Ingredients

1 loaf French bread (or you can bake your own)

1 lb spaghetti pasta

2 (29 oz) cans Hunt's tomato sauce

1 lb package grass-fed ground beef

Italian seasoning to taste

A few tablespoons of olive oil (or whichever kind you prefer or have in your pantry)

Granulated or powdered garlic to taste

Granulated or powdered onion to taste

Salt to taste

Directions

Saute ground beef in pan with a little oil.

Add about 1 teaspoon each of garlic powder, onion powder, and Italian seasoning to the beef and cook until no longer pink or raw. You can drain the oil if you'd like, I usually do not.

Add Hunt's tomato sauce and add more garlic, onion, Italian seasoning, and salt to taste.

Simmer on very low for an hour.

Toward the end, cook pasta according to package directions, adding some olive oil and salt to the boiling water to prevent stickiness.

Serve sauce over pasta and add a nice hunk of French bread on the side.

Tuna Casserole

Ingredients

1 bag egg noodles

1 can tuna

1 can cream of mushroom

1 can cream of chicken

1Tbsp chicken bouillon

1 ½ cups milk (add more if it seems too thick)

2 cups grated cheddar cheese, or use what you prefer or have on hand

Directions

In a large pan, simmer milk, tuna, cream of mushroom, cream of chicken, and chicken bouillon (this is your sauce).

Next, boil pasta until al dente.

Put pasta in a casserole dish and pour sauce over it.

Sprinkle cheese on top.

Bake for about 35 minutes at 350 degrees Fahrenheit.

You can double or triple this recipe to feed a larger family. I double this for the four of us and to have lunch to pack for my husband.

Vegan Pizza

Ingredients

Pizza dough (recipe follows)

Spaghetti sauce or tomato sauce

Daiya mozzarella cheese (vegan alternative)

Canned black olives without pits

Tomatoes

Bell pepper

Red onions

Any other vegetables you like

Dough (source: www.chef-in-training.com, but I've simplified it)

Ingredients

2 cups warm water

1 Tbsp yeast

1 Tbsp salt (optional)

5 cups flour

Directions

Mix yeast with water and let it sit for 10 minutes.

Add flour and mix, pour out onto floured surface and knead, adding more flour if necessary.

Make into a ball and return to bowl, cover with a kitchen towel and let rest for up to 20 minutes.

Divide into two parts, roll into a ball and roll out for your pizza.

Slice vegetables thinly and chop up olives.

Spread sauce with the back of a spoon and sprinkle a thin layer of vegan cheese.

Layer on vegetables.

Bake for 14 minutes at 400 degrees Fahrenheit, or until pizza is light brown and bubbly.

Briar Rabbit Burritos (This is a Briar Patch Co-op vegan vegetable wrap)

With this one you can add or omit any vegetables you like and use vegan mayo, cream cheese (vegan or dairy), or hummus.

Ingredients

Large tortillas (wheat, white flour, or flavored such as tomato basil, spinach, etc.)

Mayo, hummus, and/or cream cheese (vegan or not)

Sprouts

Bell peppers

Tomatoes

Shredded carrots

Peppers

Spinach or lettuce

Cucumbers

Pickles

Directions

Lay out the tortilla and spread on the hummus, mayo, or cream cheese.

Add vegetables (any vegetable you like or is in season) in layers and add salt and pepper to taste.

Roll up like a burrito, cut in half, and devour.

Cooking Rice

If you have a rice cooker it is simply two parts water to one part rice (white or brown). If you have no rice cooker, then add rice and water to a pot and cover, simmer on low for around 20 minutes for white rice and 40 minutes for brown.

I like to add chicken bouillon to flavor my rice. You can add butter, herbs, and other seasonings. Knorr soup packages make it a bit Rice-A-Roni-ish.

Large Pans of Delicious Veggies

Ingredients

Garlic

Red or yellow onions

Bags of frozen vegetables of your choice

Olive oil (or whichever kind you prefer or have in your pantry)

Salt and pepper

Method

These vegetables can be cooked in a regular pan, or you can use a cast iron pan, if you have one. If you use the latter, heat the pan slowly and then add plenty of oil and heat that slowly as well.

Slice a few cloves of garlic and slice up a whole onion and add both to the pan and saute until onions are beginning to brown a bit.

Add frozen vegetables and saute for as long as it takes to heat through.

I stir now and then and don't fret it they look a bit grilled.

I love using the mixed vegetables with peas, corn, green beans and carrots, and a bag of various green beans, wax beans and carrots.

Serve over rice.

You can add a little Veri Veri Teriyaki or any sauce, gravy, or eat as is. I also love this with macaroni and cheese. I just serve it side by side. So delicious and filling.

Baked Potato Fries

This method is a bit healthier than frying in oil.

Ingredients

Potatoes of your choice (we prefer Idaho russets)

Oil

Seasoning of your choice (garlic, salt, french fry seasoning, etc.)

Method

Wash and slice up your potatoes into steak fries sizes.

Toss with some oil and spread out on cookie sheets.

Sprinkle seasonings.

Bake at 400 degrees Fahrenheit for approximately 30 minutes.

They won't cook evenly, so just keep checking and when they are golden on the edges, taste one.

Slow Cooker Pot Roast

Ingredients

1 package of roasting meat, approximately 3-4 pounds

1 can cream of mushroom

1 packet of onion soup mix

5-6 potatoes chopped into small chunks

5-6 carrots chopped into small chunks

Any other vegetables you like (I love to use frozen corn and peas)

Directions

In a slow cooker, add everything plus enough water to cover.

Cook on low for 6-8 hours, or on high for 4-6 hours.

I usually double this recipe and have plenty for a couple days' worth of lunches and dinners.

Vegan Garden Pie (knockoff of Shepherd's pie, but my way)

Ingredients

1 can mushroom gravy, or any gravy (sometimes I use cream of mushroom as well)

1 package of Lightlife Smart Ground Crumbles or TVP sauteed in vegetable broth

1 lb bag of frozen peas and corn

½ onion, diced

Potatoes or potato flakes

Soy milk

Vegan butter

Oil

1 tsp garlic powder

1 tsp onion powder

Salt and pepper to taste

Directions

In a large skillet, saute onions in a bit of oil for about 5 minutes, or until translucent.

Add crumbles or the reconstituted TVP.

Add gravy and a bag of frozen vegetables and cook until heated through.

Next, add the garlic and onion powder, salt and pepper.

In a separate pot, boil potatoes, then drain, mash, add butter, salt and soy milk.

You can also just boil water to make your powdered potatoes and cook according to package directions.

Spread potatoes on top of meat substitute and vegetable mixture and put in the oven to bake for 35 minutes at 350 degrees Fahrenheit.

I always double this recipe.

Minestrone Soup (source: *Simply Sara Kitchen* on YouTube)

Ingredients

2 Tbsp oil

2 Tbsp butter

1 onion, chopped

2 stalks celery, chopped

2 to 3 zucchini, chopped

4 tomatoes, chopped

4 to 5 cloves garlic, minced

1 (15 oz) can cannellini beans

1 (15 oz) can kidney beans

1 (15 oz) can black beans

4 cups water

1 cup frozen green beans

Handful of shredded carrots

1 Tbsp tomato paste

3 cups tomato juice

2 Tbsp vegetable bouillon

2 tsp parsley

1 tsp oregano

1 tsp basil

½ tsp thyme

Salt and pepper to taste

1 bag fresh spinach

Chunk of parmesan cheese

1 ¼ cup pasta shells

Directions

In a large skillet, saute butter, oil, onion, celery, zucchini, and tomatoes.

Add garlic and cook for 1 minute.

Drain canned beans and add to skillet.

Add water, green beans, carrots, tomato paste, tomato juice, bouillon, herbs, salt, and pepper.

Stir well.

Add a few pieces of parmesan cheese and let it simmer for a while.

Add 1 ¼ cup pasta shells and cook until tender, about 7 minutes.

Next, add a bagful of fresh spinach.

This soup is SO delicious! It really does taste like Olive Garden's version, or better.

Potato and/or Salad Bar

This is for those days when you want filling, healthy food but in a self-serve style. I just bake up potatoes, shred a huge bowl of lettuce and put out small bowls and containers of whatever you would put on a salad or potato along with bottles of dressings and sauces. You can have anything you fancy, but here are some ideas for toppings:

For potatoes:

Sour cream

Butter

Chives

Cheese

Canned chili

Tomatoes

Broccoli

Cheese sauce

For salad:

Tomatoes

Canned kidney and/or garbanzo beans

Onions

Olives

Cucumbers

Sprouts

Cheese

Cabbage

Garbage Salad

Ingredients

Lettuce

Shredded carrots

Kidney beans

Tomatoes, chopped

Onions, chopped

Olives, chopped

Ground beef or turkey, cooked and cooled (optional)

Homemade ranch dressing with taco seasoning mixed in

Shredded cheddar cheese

Nacho Cheese Doritos (or Fritos Corn Chips, if you prefer)

Method

Shred a huge bowl of lettuce and add everything but the dressing and cheese until the very last moment. Crumble chips on top.

This was a friend's recipe, but I think many know this one. I turned it into a bit of a nacho salad. I love making the packets of ranch using whole fat buttermilk and mayo. Then I add packet taco seasoning to taste.

Punjabi Bean or Lentil Soup (Bali's recipe)

If you learn to make these sautes you can make all sorts of bean and lentil soups. You can also cook meats in these sautes.

Ingredients

1 pound of any kind of beans or lentils, dry

1 onion (red or yellow)

1 pepper (we use mild peppers)

3 or more cloves of garlic

1 ounce fresh ginger

2 tomatoes, chopped

1 cup fresh cilantro, chopped

1 tsp coriander seeds

1 tsp cumin seeds

1 tsp turmeric

1 Tbsp masala seasoning (There are masalas for beans and meats. They are small boxes of mixed seasonings you can find in the Indian foods section of the grocery store or at Indian food stores. You can even find them on www.amazon.com.)

Oil

Salt and pepper to taste

Directions

In a large pot, add washed beans or lentils of choice.

Add water until there are two inches of water above the beans/lentils and begin to simmer on medium heat.

Add turmeric.

Chop up all the vegetables and add half an onion and one tomato to the soup in the beginning.

Add half a teaspoon of pepper and full teaspoon of salt, about a teaspoon of oil, and a few minced cloves of garlic.

In a skillet add a tablespoon of oil, coriander and cumin, and toast for a minute or two.

Next, add remaining garlic, onions, tomatoes, and peppers.

Saute for about 2-3 minutes.

Add a heaping teaspoon of masala, then saute and cook for a few more minutes, or until vegetables are soft.

Add cooked vegetable mixture to pot of cooked beans or lentils.

Add cilantro at the end.

Peanut Butter Cookies (source: www.myrecipes.com)

I love this recipe because it's cheap. I always have the ingredients on hand and it takes just minutes.

Ingredients

1 cup peanut butter

1 cup sugar

1 egg

1 tsp vanilla extract

(Nuts, raisins, and chocolate chips are all optional)

Directions

Mix all ingredients and spoon globs onto a cookie sheet, about two inches apart.

Bake for 10 to 15 minutes at 325 degrees Fahrenheit.

I always double the batch!

Easiest Cheesecake Ever

This is a no bake, super easy, and so good recipe. I have no idea where I got it from.

Ingredients

1 store bought graham cracker crust

8 oz cream cheese

1/3 cup sugar

2 tsp vanilla extract

1 cup sour cream

Directions

Use a beater to mix cream cheese, sugar, vanilla extract, and sour cream.

Pour into graham cracker pie crust.

Chill in fridge for at least 4 hours to allow it to set.

Homemade Sugar-Free Lemonade

Ingredients

Water

Lemons

Stevia (you can also use real sugar, honey, or maple syrup, but then it won't be sugar-free)

Method

In a pitcher filled with water, add as much squeezed lemon juice and Stevia as you like.

Keep adding sweetener and lemon juice until it tastes yummy.

Moon Beam Tea (source: *The Help Yourself Cookbook for Kids: 60 Easy Plant-Based Recipes Kids Can Make to Stay Healthy and Save the Earth* by Ruby Roth)

Ingredients

Hot water

Chamomile tea

Honey, agave, or sugar

Milk or plant milk

Method

Brew tea in hot water.

Add sweetener and milk of choice to taste.

The kids love this tea and I drink it at night.

Cranberry Water

Ingredients

Water

Cranberry juice

Ice

Method

Add 1 part cranberry juice to 3 parts water.

Serve over ice.

This is a great way to get kids to drink more water in the summer. I usually use pure cranberry juice without sugar and add Stevia to it.

Homemade Yogurt

Ingredients

1 gallon of milk

1 cup of yogurt (you can use some from your previous batch or buy at the store if you are just starting out)

Directions

Add milk to a large Dutch oven or any pot with a tight-fitting lid.

Simmer slowly until temperature reaches 200 degrees Fahrenheit.

Remove from heat and let cool to 115 degrees Fahrenheit.

Turn oven on to preheat for about 10 minutes.

In a separate bowl, combine 2 cups of heated milk with 1 cup of yogurt.

Whisk gently and add back to Dutch oven or pot and stir to combine.

Place in turned off oven and leave overnight.

If it doesn't firm up, let sit for a few more hours. The house and/or oven must be warm. This allows it to solidify with all the good bacteria and cultures. This is so healthy, and the cost is $1 for a big container instead of $5 or more for organic yogurt at the grocery store.

Vegan Chocolate Cake (this sounds funky, but it is better than regular cake)

Ingredients

2 ½ cups white flour

¾ cup to 1 cup cocoa

2 tsp salt

2 tsp baking soda

2 cups honey

1 cup coconut oil

1 cup water

1 cup almond milk or soy milk

2 tsp vanilla extract (you can substitute and use any other preferred extract such as maple, coconut, etc.)

Directions

Preheat oven to 350 degrees Fahrenheit.

In a large bowl, mix together flour, cocoa, salt, and baking soda.

Add honey, coconut oil, water, milk, and vanilla extract.

Mix until combined.

Pour into a 9-inch cake pan and bake for 35 minutes, or until toothpick inserted in the center comes out clean.

Frosting

Ingredients

4 oz dark chocolate (you can use milk chocolate, but then it won't be vegan)

2 Tbsp coconut oil

1/3 cup water

Directions

In a medium saucepan, add chocolate, coconut oil, and water.

On low to medium heat, stir frequently until melted. Pour on top of cake.

Whole Wheat Pizza Crust

Ingredients

1 tsp sugar

1 ½ cups warm water

1 Tbsp active dry yeast

1 Tbsp olive oil

1 tsp salt

2 cups whole wheat flour

1 ½ cups white flour

Directions

In a large bowl, dissolve sugar in warm water.

Sprinkle yeast on top.

Let stand for 10 minutes.

Stir in olive oil, salt, whole wheat flour, and 1 cup of white flour.

Pour out onto clean, floured surface and knead in remaining white flour until dough becomes smooth.

Place in oiled bowl, lightly coating dough.

Cover with towel and let stand for 1 hour.

After 1 hour, your dough should be doubled. Place dough on floured surface and divide into two parts.

Form into tight balls and let rise for 45 more

minutes.

Oil pizza pans. Roll out and stretch to fit pans and load with desired sauce and toppings.
I just use Hunt's tomato sauce with extra garlic powder and Italian seasoning as my sauce.

Bake at 425 degrees Fahrenheit for 14 to 20 minutes. Yummy.

Mom's Spaghetti Sauce (this was my mother's sauce from what I remember, with a few things added or taken out)

Ingredients

Hunt's cans of tomato sauce (very inexpensive)

Ground beef

Ground pork sausage

Green bell pepper, finely chopped

Italian seasoning

Freshly chopped garlic or granulated/powdered

garlic

Directions

In a large pot, brown meat until fully cooked.

Add sauce, bell pepper, and seasonings.

Simmer on low heat for about an hour or so.

The longer it simmers on very low heat, the more flavorful the sauce. You can make your own tomato sauce, as well.

Homemade Tomato Sauce (This is from *Dump Dinners*, with some added ingredients)

Ingredients

Tomatoes (very ripe)

Onions

Salt

Butter

Italian seasoning

Garlic

Directions

In a large pot, simmer for one hour.

When cooled, blend and store in refrigerator.

Vegetarian Black Bean Enchiladas

This is my own little creation. This dish is so good!

Ingredients

Black beans, homemade or store-bought

White rice, cooked with chicken bouillon, preferably

Cheese (mild cheddar, jalapeno cheddar, or cotija)

Corn tortillas

Green enchilada sauce, canned

Butter

Directions

In a large skillet, heat up a stack of corn tortillas with a touch of butter, until they are soft and pliable. Set aside.

Grease a casserole pan.

Have all three cheeses shredded and mixed on a big plate.

Place tortillas side by side in pan.

Fill with beans and cheese and roll.

Arrange side by side.

When pan is full, sprinkle cheese and pour the can of enchilada sauce on top. Sprinkle more cheese.

Bake at 350 degrees Fahrenheit for 35 to 40 minutes.

Serve with white rice and beans on the side. You can use plain water or vegetable stock to cook the rice, if you prefer. Yahoo, it's good!

Frozen Bean and Cheese Burritos

Ingredients

Pinto or black beans, cooked

Rice, cooked

Cheese

Tortillas

Butter (optional)

Directions

In a big pot, mix desired amount of rice, beans, shredded cheese, and any seasonings you like. Granulated garlic and onion work great here.

When everything is mixed well and cheese is melted, scoop into a large tortilla and fold to make burritos. Avoid overfilling.

Place all burritos seam side down on a greased cookie sheet.

Lightly brush tops with melted butter.

Bake at 350 degrees Fahrenheit for 20 to 25 minutes, or until golden brown.

Be sure to keep an eye on them so they don't burn.

Enjoy and freeze the rest.

These are delicious, much better than the store

bought (because they actually have substantial amounts of beans and rice), and you can just take one or two out of the freezer and microwave to reheat. I make tons at a time.

Down-Home Chicken Soup

Ingredients

3-5 lbs bone-in chicken (whole, thighs, or legs)

Vegetables (all kinds)

Chicken bouillon

Italian seasoning or a combination of basil and oregano

Salt

½ lb egg noodles or pasta, cooked (rice or barley are fine, too)

Directions

Place chicken in a large pot.

Add water to cover.

Cook on low to medium heat for 1 ½ to 2 hours, or until internal temperature reaches 165 degrees Fahrenheit.

Once cool enough to handle, transfer chicken to

platter to debone.

Return to pot, add bouillon, seasonings, and salt to taste.

Simmer for approximately 15-20 minutes more.

Add desired vegetables and continue to simmer until they are soft.

Add cooked egg noodles or pasta and serve.

You may use rice or barley instead. Pasta and rice get mushy in soup after some time. Egg noodles are the best for this soup. You can also just use chicken and vegetables and serve with some freshly baked bread.

Atta Flatbread

Ingredients

2 cups atta flour

1 cup water

3-4 Tbsp butter

This is what I call an Indian tortilla.

Directions

In a large bowl, add the flour and water and mix to

form a dough.

Make into small balls.

On a floured surface, roll out each one.

Add a pat of butter (approximately ½ tablespoon) to hot pan.

Cook each flatbread for about 30-45 seconds per side. Serve warm.

Wheat and white atta flour can be found at Indian grocery stores, the international foods aisle at some grocery stores, and online. Buy a big bag and keep it on hand for these delicious flatbreads.

We eat this with everything. His curry chicken, my black beans.

Cheap and Easy Snack Ideas

Snacking is fun and can be nutritious, so I like to make healthy snack plates. Sometimes my kids and I just graze throughout the day and then eat a proper meal in the evening with Bali.

- Cheese and raisins
- Homemade raw granola bars made with oats, nuts, seeds, nut butters, and raisins (great recipes can be found online)
- Olives and pickles
- Organic yogurt loaded with probiotics (try plain Greek and add berries or make your own)
- Sliced and/or chopped fruit with nut butters

- Vegetables with peanut butter or hummus
- Seeds, nuts, and dried fruit
- Popcorn with coconut oil, nutritional yeast, and salt
- Homemade sliced bread with jam, nut butters, or cheese
- Sprouts
- Shredded carrots and red cabbage with a little ranch or dressing of your choice
- Salad (most kids actually like salad and if they say they don't, just keep serving it, trying different dressings, and they will eventually)

Make your own versions of frozen convenience foods. I make frozen lasagnas, frozen cheese, bean, and rice burritos, frozen enchiladas, and so much more. Just cook a double or triple batch of lasagna, soup, or casseroles, and freeze the extra.

Substitutions For Name Brand Convenience Foods (some of these recipes are from *The Complete Tightwad Gazette*)

Cocoa Mix

Ingredients

10 cups powdered milk

6 oz non-dairy creamer

1 lb Nestle Nesquik Chocolate Milk Powder

1/3 cup confectioners' sugar

Directions

Mix well. Store in airtight container in a cool, dry place.

Shake 'n Bake (remember this oldie, but goodie?)

Ingredients

4 cups flour

4 cups crushed saltine crackers

4 Tbsp salt

2 tsp onion powder

3 Tbsp paprika

Directions

Mix well. Store in airtight container in a cool, dry place.

Raisin Oatmeal Scones

Ingredients

1 ½ cups flour

1 cup dry oatmeal

1 tsp baking soda

½ tsp salt

¼ cup margarine

½ cup raisins

¾ cup sour milk (milk with 2 tsp vinegar)

1 egg, beaten

Directions

Preheat oven to 400 degrees Fahrenheit.

In a large bowl, mix flour, oatmeal, baking soda, salt, margarine, raisins, and sour milk until all ingredients are combined.

Roll out to approximately 3/4 inch thick, and cut into squares or shapes.

Place on large cookie sheet. Bake for 10 minutes.

Remove from oven, glaze with beaten egg, and bake for 5 more minutes, or until golden brown.

Seasoned Salt

Ingredients

8 Tbsp salt

3 Tbsp black pepper

2 Tbsp paprika

½ tsp onion powder

½ tsp garlic powder

Directions

Mix well. Store in airtight container in a cool, dry place.

Taco Seasoning

Ingredients

6 tsp chili powder

4 ½ tsp cumin

5 tsp paprika

3 tsp onion powder

2 ½ tsp garlic powder

¼ tsp cayenne pepper powder

Directions

Mix well. Store in airtight container in a cool, dry place.

Onion Soup Mix

Ingredients

¾ cup dried, minced onion

4 tsp onion powder

1/3 cup beef bouillon powder

¼ tsp ground celery seeds

¼ tsp sugar

Directions

Mix well. Store in airtight container in a cool, dry place.

Seasoned Rice Mix

Ingredients

3 cups uncooked rice

¼ cup dried parsley flakes

6 Tbsp chicken or beef bouillon powder

2 tsp onion powder

½ tsp garlic powder

½ tsp dried thyme

Directions

Mix well and store in airtight container in a cool, dry place.

Cook as you would normally cook rice.

Country Biscuit Mix

Ingredients

10 cups flour

⅓ cup baking powder

1 Tbsp salt

2 cups shortening

Directions

Using a food processor or pastry cutter, mix well to make sure shortening is evenly distributed.

Store in airtight container. Lasts 1 to 6 months at room temperature, during colder weather.

You may also refrigerate. Use it the same way you would use Bisquick.

Meatless Monday Casserole

Ingredients

3 cups vegetable broth

¾ cups uncooked lentils

½ cup uncooked brown rice

¾ cup onion, chopped

½ tsp sweet basil

¼ tsp oregano

¼ tsp thyme

¼ tsp garlic powder

1 ½ cups shredded cheese (use your favorite)

Directions

Add all ingredients (except cheese) to a baking dish and mix.

Cover and bake at 375 degrees Fahrenheit for approximately 1 ½ hours, stirring once halfway through the cooking time.

Sprinkle cheese and return to oven for an additional 10 minutes, or until it has melted and is golden and bubbly.

Remove from oven and let cool for another 10 minutes before serving.

YouTube Cooking Channels

Pro Home Cooks

As mentioned previously, this used to be *Brothers Green Eats* but the brothers have gone their separate ways. The older brother, Mike took over the channel. He is so talented. All the old videos are still on there and they are very fun to watch and learn from. You can learn how to make everything, and I mean EVERYTHING: Japanese, Chinese takeout, bagels, sourdough, Indian street sandwiches, sauces, kombuchas, simple food for work lunches, budget meals, fancy dishes, and on and on. You can even learn about canning! **This is my favorite channel.**

You Enjoy Life

This is the younger brother, Josh's new channel. This is a great one for healthy and super affordable meals.

Simply Sara Kitchen

I love her older recipes and have tried many. They are always easy and fantastic. Her vegan corn dogs, minestrone soup, mushroom stroganoff, crab rangoons, and buckeye balls are repeats for sure.

Homestead Tessie

Tessie and her husband live in a fixed up mobile home on one acre of land that they have turned into a farm, complete with gardens and chickens. In addition to growing much of their produce, she has amazing ways to make the food budget stretch and find free food without taking from those in need.

Jan Creson

This is a great one for those of you who love Dollar Tree shopping. She makes some pretty creative dishes with ingredients that were all purchased at Dollar Tree.

A More Plant-Based Kitchen

I went a whole year cultivating an almost entirely vegan diet, and I just adored every moment of it. I loved the vegan cooking channels on YouTube. I learned all I could about vegan nutrition and how to veganize all the meat- and dairy-based dishes we love. This is where my true creativity in the kitchen blossomed.

I prefer to call it a more plant-based diet these days because being vegan is a very big undertaking that goes beyond food. It is a diet supporting the kindness and well-being of all living things. This can be as extreme as not consuming honey and not wearing wool.

We don't stick to that way of eating 100% of the time, as I do let my boys eat what they crave for I feel that they need a well-rounded diet while they are growing. We actually like meat but not the cruelty connected to raising it. I do use honey, wear wool, and have old Ugg boots, and a sheepskin rug from long ago. We also go deep into being vegetarian (excluding dairy), and then we have the occasional day we bake up a chicken. We are not committed to any one way of eating.

However, after watching all the documentaries such as *Food Matters, In Defense of Food, Forks Over Knives, Farmaggedon, Vegucated, Fat, Sick, and Nearly Dead, Super Size Me*, and many more…well, you never eat the same, really.

When we eat meat and dairy we buy it without hormones or antibiotics. We stick to free-range, Certified Humane Raised & Handled, and as local as possible. My conscience still bothers me, and it isn't long before my kitchen goes back to animal-free and overflowing with the bounties of the earth.

According to Global Data (www.globaldata.com), veganism grew by 600% between 2014 and 2017. Fast food restaurants are jumping in. Carl's Jr. has a new meatless burger they call The Beyond Burger. Burger King has the Impossible Whopper. They wave their banners proudly and I just can't wait for payday so I can have a vegan Whopper. Yes!

Other good documentaries are *Earthlings, Meet Your Meat, The Ghosts In Our Machine, and Cowspiracy: The Sustainability Secret*.

How to Prepare Your Pantry for a Vegan or Plant-Based Life

There are two ways to do it. You can ease into it and use up what you have in your pantries or jump right in and donate things to the food bank or neighborhood.

Here are the foods I keep stocked on my shelves and in the refrigerator and freezer:

Dry goods

White flour
Wheat flour
Oats, old fashioned
Steel cut oats
Black beans
Pinto beans
Garbanzo beans
Brown lentils
Red lentils
Walnuts
Cashews
Almonds
Brown rice
White rice
Coffee
Nut butters
Black olives, canned (think pizza)

Baking Supplies

Baking powder
Baking soda
Ground cinnamon
Vanilla extract
Nutmeg
Ground ginger
Date syrup
Coconut sugar
Powdered sugar

Cacao powder (not to be confused with cocoa)
Maple syrup

Gluten-free mixes are also good to keep on hand if you have issues, or just prefer them. Bob's Red Mill makes gluten-free mixes for pancakes, pizza crust, cornbread, and more.

Seasonings and Sauces

Sriracha
Himalayan pink salt
Ground black pepper
Ground white pepper
Italian seasoning
Fennel powder
Cayenne powder
Tajin (with an added squeeze of lime juice, this is great on fruit)
Garlic powder
Onion powder
Turmeric
Masala
Nutritional yeast
Vinegars: white, rice, and wine
Coconut oil
Sesame oil
Olive oil

Frozen Goods

Lots of veggies and greens
Berries
Bananas
Quorn Meatless & Soy Free Turk'y Roast
Veggie burgers (Amy's, Boca, Quorn, Gardein...so many to try!)

Veggie hot dogs
Hot dog buns
Hamburger buns

Refrigerator

Ketchup (Organicville is a good one)
Relish
Mustard
Coconut aminos
Greens
Vegetables
Fruit
Plant-based milks
Earth Balance butter or plant-based butters
Vegenaise
Annie's salad dressings (read the label, not all are vegan)
Vegan ranch dressing (Follow Your Heart is a good brand)
Hoisin Sauce
Chili garlic sauce
Sweet chili sauce
Pickles (whole dill and sliced bread and butter)
Olives (whatever you like, we love garlic stuffed)

Baskets

Potatoes: Yukon Gold, Idaho russets, red, sweet, and purple
Tomatoes
Avocados
Ginger
Onions
Garlic
Lemons and limes

Going Organic on a Budget

I won't sugarcoat it. Eating healthy is very expensive. However, in the end it will save your health, a retirement fund spent in doctors' offices, and picking up prescriptions at Walmart pharmacies. It will be the difference between being a sick, fat old person and being a fit, active, healthy, and spirited elder.

Farmers used to garden and raise animals organically in the olden days, and people didn't have the diseases they have today. Our society did not suffer from as much depression, mental illness, obesity, cancer, or other maladies that we see today. All I can think is that all the poisons we spray on crops permeate the food, soil, groundwater (eventually), and air; and we are eating, drinking, and breathing it.

It's not good for Mother Earth and it's certainly not what God would intend for us, except to learn that poisons will be our demise in the end.

But how do we afford good food when we are on fixed incomes and/or food stamps? Sometimes we just can't, and I get that. My hope is that as the organic movement grows, it will become more affordable.

In addition to buying in bulk and joining a co-op to help offset the high costs of organic foods, something that you can do in the meantime is purchase your produce in season and from the Clean 15 and Dirty Dozen lists:

The lists for 2019 are as follows:

Clean Fifteen

1. Avocados

2. Sweet corn

3. Pineapples

4. Frozen sweet peas

5. Onions

6. Papayas

7. Eggplants

8. Asparagus

9. Kiwis

10. Cabbages

11. Cauliflower

12. Cantaloupes

13. Broccoli

14. Mushrooms

15. Honeydew melons

Dirty Dozen

1. Strawberries

2. Spinach

3. Kale

4. Nectarines

5. Apples

6. Grapes

7. Peaches

8. Cherries

9. Pears

10. Tomatoes

11. Celery

12. Potatoes

There are plenty of things that are safe and not organic. Also, cooking simple foods at home will cut costs and free up some money to go toward the additional price of organics.

Chapter 5

Delicious Vegan Recipes to Get You Started

I first tried veganism when I was 15 years old. I went to an activist summer camp where I met Ram Dass and Ben and Jerry (they now make lots of vegan ice cream). I learned about walking meditations and the pleasure of not eating animals. That was over 30 years ago, and unfortunately, as a vegan, your choices were salad and tofu. It wasn't popular like it is now, and people feared protein deficiencies.

Today, it is *so* easy to eat plant-based. There are cookbooks and YouTube chefs galore! There are so many fun foods out there that will make your diehard meat-eating dreams come true, and it can all happen with some creative bean and walnut combos.

Beware: you can become a junk food vegan quickly. The processed food will be a step up from the real meat and cheese processed foods, but if you want to feel clean from the inside and filled with light and energy, learn to make your own foods from scratch.

It is important for the family, especially the children, to have meals packed with nutrition, so that they really benefit from this new lifestyle. The skin will clear up, the weight will come off. Patience is required, and you can eat to your heart's content.

Here are some dishes I have found on the YouTube circuit. I will list all my favorite vegan cooking channels at the end of this chapter, so you can go right on YouTube and watch the videos yourself. *High Carb Hannah* and *Chef AJ* don't do salt; I do. I also like a lot of garlic and not so much the cayenne. Have fun with the recipes and make them your own.

Lentil Loaf (source: *High Carb Hannah* on YouTube)

This is delicious. I'm fond of real meatloaf, so I was sure this would not pass the test. It did. This lentil loaf with ketchup and mashed potatoes is a dream. Add some peas or corn to really make it a plateful of winter comfort food.

Ingredients

1 cup brown lentils

½ cup red lentils

1 ½ cups oat flour (just ground oats)

3 cups plus 6 Tbsp water

1 carrot, chopped

2 stalks celery, chopped

1 bell pepper, any color (I like green, and it's less

pricey), diced

½ medium onion (red or yellow if you prefer), finely

diced

1 Tbsp fennel powder

1 Tbsp Italian seasoning

1 Tbsp onion powder

3 Tbsp ground flax seeds

1 tsp cayenne (optional)

I like to add 1 Tbsp garlic powder and 1 Tbsp salt

Directions

In a medium to large pot, mix brown and red lentils with diced onion, celery, carrot, bell pepper, and 3 cups water.

Bring to boil.

Reduce heat to simmer until lentils are soft. It's okay if there is a little water but most should be evaporated. I'd say twenty to thirty minutes. I usually just keep an eye on it.

In a small bowl, mix ground flax seeds with 6 tablespoons of water. Let sit while the lentils and vegetables cook. This is going to get gelatinous and be your binder.

In a separate bowl, mix all the seasonings: fennel, Italian seasoning, garlic and onion powder, and salt if you like. You can even add pepper and other seasonings. Play with it.

Grind the oats in a blender to make the flour.

When lentils and vegetables are cooked, add the oat flour, seasonings, and flax mixture.

Mix well and divide. Form into loaves. Place into 2 nonstick pans.

Bake at 350 degrees Fahrenheit for approximately 30-45 minutes.

Note: After about 20 minutes, remove from oven, add about ¼ cup of ketchup to each loaf and return to oven to finish baking.

Makes 2 loaves.

Mashed Potatoes

Ingredients

Potatoes (any potato will do, but Yukon gold is the

richest and yummiest in this dish)

Plain, unsweetened soy milk

Vegan butter (optional)

Salt and pepper to taste

Nutritional yeast

Granulated or powdered onion

Granulated or powdered garlic

Method

In a large pot, boil potatoes until tender.

Drain and return to pot.

Add all remaining ingredients, and use a hand mixer to whip them to a creamy texture.

You can add even more seasonings if you're feeling daring.

Corn and Brussels Sprouts

My kids love this! I love this! You can substitute vegetable broth for the oil and butter.

Ingredients

Frozen corn

Fresh brussels sprouts

Earth Balance vegan butter

Coconut oil

Garlic

Salt

White pepper

Method

In a large pan, saute garlic in coconut oil and butter.

Don't toast or burn, just heat to release the essence of the garlic. Add frozen corn.

Wash and cut brussels sprouts in half and add to pan. Don't cook them too long.

Add more butter, salt and pepper. Serve.

Vegan Tostadas From Heaven

This dish is so easy and fast.

Ingredients

Homemade or canned refried beans (I sometimes

add my favorite canned beans: Ranch Style Beans

and S&W Chili Beans)

Tostadas

Lettuce

Tomatoes

Homemade vegan thousand island dressing

Sriracha

Method

I usually make refried beans and throw in a can of the S&W Chili and Ranch Style beans to make it fabulous. Mash it all up.

Top tostadas with beans, shredded lettuce, chopped tomatoes and then drizzle generously with thousand island dressing and Sriracha.

Homemade Vegan Thousand Island

I combined three different recipes here. There is Worcestershire sauce in mine and that is not vegan (I was disappointed). But there is a vegan substitute, yay!

Ingredients

1 cup Vegenaise

1 Tbsp Annie's Worcestershire sauce (vegan, baby!)

2 Tbsp ketchup

1 Tbsp lemon juice (fresh)

2 Tbsp relish

1 Tbsp minced garlic (jarred is best for strong flavor)

1 Tbsp red onion, minced

Salt to taste

White pepper to taste

Vinegar is optional (I don't use it)

Directions

In a large bowl, mix all ingredients until combined.

Store in a jar and keep refrigerated.

It gets better each day, as the flavors marinate. I sort of eyeball the measurements and add to taste, so this is truly a foundation recipe. Experiment to make it to your liking. Add more lemon or pepper, if you wish. You can even spice it up with a little Sriracha.

Sometimes I just drizzle this dressing on lettuce leaves and eat them like an appetizer. I eat a head of lettuce almost daily.

Martha Stewart's One Pot Pasta

I used to make this when we used chicken broth and it was incredibly delicious. I now just use vegetable broth instead. The recipe calls for water, but I find that a broth makes it 10 times yummier.

Ingredients

12 oz linguine pasta

1 onion, chopped

½ tsp pepper flakes

2 Tbsp olive oil

4 ½ cups vegetable broth

12 oz cherry or grape tomatoes, chopped in half or

quartered

4 cloves fresh garlic, minced

2 sprigs basil

Salt and pepper to taste

Directions

Place all ingredients in a pot and bring to a boil.

Reduce heat and stir occasionally until all the water or broth is absorbed by the pasta.

Stovetop Vegan Pizza

This is a dish is a combination of recipes. Both *High Carb Hannah* and Nikki over at www.chef-in-training.com have versions, but you may top it however you like. This dish works well with my gas stove; it seems easier to make, and I love the thick, pan style.

There are a few parts to this pizza.

The Perfect Pizza Dough (source: www.chef-in-training.com)

Ingredients

2 cups warm water

1 Tbsp active dry yeast

1 Tbsp salt

5 cups flour

Directions

Add yeast to warm water and let sit for 5 minutes.

Add half the flour and mix well, pour onto floured board and mix in remainder.

Knead and return to bowl to sit covered with a towel for 20 minutes.

She gets a bit fancier, but I find simple works as well.

Pizza Assembly

Method

Sprinkle cornmeal on bottom of a large skillet.

Press dough into the pan to completely cover the bottom.

Add sauce and toppings of your choice.

We love tons of olives, corn, red onions, and pineapple. Go easy on sliced tomatoes if you decide to use them, as they make the dough soggy. Be careful not to use too much sauce for this same reason.

If you would like a vegan cheese, *High Carb Hannah* has a good recipe for one:

Ingredients

¼ cup cashews

3 Tbsp nutritional yeast

½ Tbsp Granulated or powdered garlic, or to taste

Himalayan pink salt, to taste

Directions

Blend all ingredients in a blender.

Sprinkle on pizza.

Place pan on stove and cover with a tight-fitting lid.

Cook on low for approximately 15 minutes. This part is tricky; sometimes it's taken up to 30 minutes if there are lots of watery toppings. Keep an eye on it.

When it is fully cooked, place it on a chopping board, cut and serve. So good.

Makes 2 pan pizzas.

Asian Noodle Soup

There is some controversy as to whether this is really considered vegan. I use a pho soup mix or wonton soup mix. The beef and chicken are artificial flavors and I've seen Rose from *Cheap Lazy Vegan* on YouTube eat artificially flavored chicken ramen. This is for you to decide. You can also just use an alternative vegan broth.

I just boil a huge pot of water with the soup seasoning, rice noodles, and tons of greens. Sometimes I get all this from our local Korean store, so I have no idea what the greens are called. We eat the soup in huge bowls that I also purchased there, and we use chopsticks because it's fun.

This is a great soup for cold days. You leave the table feeling warm, full, and fortified.

Packed Veggie Eggless Rolls

I make these now and then, and they are a hit, even with my elderly neighbors who love their meat. They are very high in fat, so this is a treat.

Ingredients

Egg roll wraps (get the soft, large ones)

Vegetables (red and green cabbage, carrots,

onions, bean sprouts)

Veri Veri Teriyaki

Oil (a light oil for frying)

Dipping sauce of choice (I use sweet chili sauce)

Water for steaming

Directions

Shred vegetables in a food processor or grate and chop by hand. You can add whatever else you would like, such as tofu or other vegetables.

In a wok or large pan, add vegetables and a bit of water. Put the lid on to steam for a short period. You want the vegetables to be cooked, but still be a bit crunchy.

Drain, return to pan, and add Veri Veri Teriyaki sauce.

Lay the wrap on a dry surface and put a large amount of vegetables in the middle, then wrap it like a burrito and seal with a dab of water. I like to make batches, so they are fresh and crunchy.

In a large, deep pan, add about an inch of oil. Let the oil get hot, but not boiling, *crazy* hot.

Use tongs to carefully add egg rolls and turn as needed until golden brown.

Place on a platter with paper towels to absorb all the oil.

Serve with dipping sauce.

You can also choose different sauces, we just like Thai sweet chili sauce.

Faux Tuna Salad (source: www.revolutioninbloom.com)

1-15 oz can cooked garbanzo beans

½ cup diced dill pickles

½ cup diced celery

½ diced red onion

1 or 2 Tbsp nori sheets ground to flakes

Vegenaise (as much as you like)

Salt to taste

Pepper to taste

Add garbanzo beans to a food processor and pulse a few times, keeping them a bit textured, and not pasty. You want a sort of flaky texture. Pour into bowl.

Mix in all remaining ingredients and you're done.

I have taken to adding other things such as mustard and fresh lemon juice. Others like cayenne or other seasonings.

This recipe is very flexible. You can adjust all the ingredients to your liking; adding more of this, and less of that. I found we liked a ton of nori flakes and extra salt. This is a very good dish to eat on crackers and in sandwiches.

I usually double the batch.

Green Smoothie

Ingredients

Frozen bananas

Frozen berries (optional)

Almond or soy milk

Greens (best for smoothies are kale, spinach,

dandelion greens, collards, and chard)

A Vitamix works best for these smoothies, but any good one will do.

Method

Start by blending the greens and milk.

Next, add bananas and frozen berries or any other fruit, one by one. Do this until it has reached the sweetness and creaminess you love.

Mangos and pineapple are good, too. You don't need to use all these greens in one smoothie.

Mix and match or just use one at a time.

Green Juice (Sometimes Red):

This recipe is very simple.

Ingredients

Apples

Fresh lemon, peeled

Fresh ginger, peeled

Cucumber

Carrots

Celery

Greens

Beets

Method

Juice all ingredients according to manufacturer's

directions.

You decide the amount of fruits and vegetables you want to juice. We like to use extra carrots and apples to make it a bit sweeter for the kids. If you are trying to detox from metals such as aluminum in vaccines, throw in cilantro and parsley each time.

Get the cheapest apples. When you juice them, it doesn't matter if they are old. See if your health food store marks down older produce. Perhaps they are willing to give it to you for compost. If so, take it home and then salvage what you can. My old co-op used to have boxes of reduced produce daily. I liked to buy bags of it and use it for juicing because even if it's bruised or funky, it all becomes juice.

Desserts and Coffee

What is life without sweets and coffee? Not much to me. Here are some vegan desserts, and one is even healthy! I'll also share my best coffee secrets.

Vegan Vanilla Cake (source: www.lovingitvegan.com)

Ingredients

1 ¾ cups all-purpose flour

1 cup sugar

1 tsp baking soda

½ tsp salt

1 cup plain soy milk

2 tsp vanilla extract

1/3 cup olive oil (I use coconut oil)

1 Tbsp white vinegar

Directions

In a large bowl, mix wet ingredients.

In another, mix dry ingredients.

Combine the two, and pour in a baking pan.
Bake in a preheated oven at 350 degrees
Fahrenheit for 30 minutes or until toothpick inserted
in the middle comes out clean.

Vegan Vanilla Buttercream Frosting (source: www.elizabethrider.com)

Ingredients

1 cup Earth Balance butter

3 cups powdered sugar

2 tsp soy or almond milk

¾ tsp vanilla extract

Note: For chocolate buttercream I replace 1 cup of powdered sugar with 1 cup of cacao powder.

Directions

Whip until creamy.

Store in refrigerator in an airtight container for up to 7 days.

CHEF AJ's Black Bean Chocolate Brownies
(source: *CHEF AJ* on YouTube)

These brownies are super healthy! I let my boys eat these some mornings for fun.

Ingredients

2 cups rinsed black beans, cooked

¾ cup oats (you can grind into flour or leave whole)

1 cup date syrup (I use Date Lady)

½ cup cocoa (I use cacao; it's healthier)

1 tsp baking powder

½ tsp baking soda

Chocolate chips, as little or as much as you want

(enjoy life!)

Directions

Place all ingredients in a food processor, pulse a few times, until combined. Pour into a baking pan. I like to use my cast iron skillet and then cover the top with dark chocolate chips. Sometimes I'll add sprinkles for fun. Bake in a preheated oven at 350 degrees Fahrenheit for 20-30 minutes, depending on the size of your pan.

Kate's Fancy Espresso Coffee

I don't drink this every day, or I'd have even more weight to lose.

Ingredients

Espresso

Milk

Water

Method

Make a strong cup of espresso in a stovetop Italian espresso maker. Pour into a large mug, add some hot water and a large scoop of Nature's Charm Sweetened Condensed Coconut Milk. This is a treat!

Use as much or as little espresso, water, and milk as you want.

I like to stock up on Boca burgers, Amy's burgers, and vegan hot dogs. However, you can find recipes to make your own burgers. Also, carrot dogs are very popular. They look good and we will be trying them soon. *High Carb Hannah* has a sweet potato and black bean burger that is easy and can be grilled on the George Foreman grill.

There is also a chewy, gooey cheese recipe on *It Doesn't Taste Like Chicken*'s website.

Vitamin Deficiencies

You may want to take extra vitamin B12 and vitamin D. These are hard to get without the processed dairy and meat.

Eating a wide variety of vegetables, fruits, grains, legumes, nuts, and seeds will cover everything else. Educate yourself so you are giving your family the best chance at having vibrant health.
Great Chefs To Keep You Inspired

Here is a list of some creative vegan chefs on YouTube to help you make amazing dishes and keep everyone happy. Even the meat eaters may find their happy place on the plate.

MommyTang
High Carb Hannah

It Doesn't Taste Like Chicken
CHEF AJ
Edgy Veg
The Veggie Nut
avantgardevegan
The Happy Pear (great for kid-friendly vegan foods)
The Vegan Zombie
Cheap Lazy Vegan (fantastic for quick, cheap, and even some junk food)
Savvy Vegan (great for gluten-free recipes including fantastic 2 ingredient bread as well as pancakes)

Chapter 6

Growing Free Organics

Dig up that lawn! Start collecting free containers from bakeries. Growing your own food is fun, creative, therapeutic, challenging (in the best way), and gives one a sense of purpose and sustainability.

It takes a few years to really learn how to grow an abundance of food, especially in a small space. The first year we had a lush garden but no produce, only two zucchini. It turned out that we had depleted soil. We then added a ton of aged horse manure and layered on compost that we had been building up and cooking all winter. This summer we had plenty of produce. If you use horse manure in your garden, be sure to let it sit in a big pile and cook for months to get rid of the E. coli and become mild.

Where we failed was not creating climbing poles and walls for the cucumbers and melons. They went rogue and covered most of the plots. Lesson learned for next year. I also grew too much of the wrong cucumber and it went wild. I planted too many cherry tomatoes when I wanted Romas and Beefsteak, and I had no idea that you actually need to prune the tomato plants all year.

Reading urban homesteading books and watching YouTube channels about gardening will somewhat prepare you. However, I have found that the best way is to jump in and learn as you go. Don't take it too seriously at first, because failure is only a season away. Always be sure to educate yourself and ask, ask, ask.

Some YouTube channels I found helpful:

Nilkanta Halder, The Indian Gardener
Hollis and Nancy's Homestead
The Rusted Garden
MIgardener

Some books to help:

Urban Homesteading: Heirloom Skills for Sustainable Living by Rachel Kaplan

Homesteading: A Backyard Guide to Growing Your Own Food, Canning, Keeping Chickens, Generating Your Own Energy, Crafting, Herbal Medicine, and More by Abigail R. Gehring

Backyard Homesteading: A Back-to-Basics Guide to Self-Sufficiency, by David Toht

Now, to start a kitchen garden, you just need a little plot. If you rent, ask the landlord for permission to dig up the lawn in the front or backyard. If you own, you do what you like. In some states you can't have a front yard garden (silly state), but in California it is now legal to have a front yard garden, use rain barrels, and have chickens. Yee-haw!

You can be downright poor and start a garden. I'll show you the poor man's way because it works for everyone, and as you have more money you can purchase more trees, seeds, and tools.

Poor Man's Tools

Shovel
Buckets (you can get them for free at bakeries or big stores with bakeries)

Soil Enhancers and Amendments

Horse, cow, or chicken manure (free at ranches, stables, and farms)
Coffee grounds (free at coffee shops if you ask and leave a bucket or two)
Compost (free because you make it)

Seeds and plants can be purchased with food stamps. I see racks filled with seeds and herb plants at WinCo Foods during growing season. Stock up. You can also get seed packets at dollar stores. They're usually priced at 4/$1.

Fruit and nut trees are cheaper the smaller they are, but it also means that it will take longer (perhaps years) before they produce fruit.

You can find free truckloads of mulch on Craigslist, or just use a $10 bale of straw from the feed store for ground cover. Straw is great when you harvest and then turn it into the soil. It makes the soil more workable over time.

Natural Pesticides

You can use blue Dawn dish soap and water in a spray bottle for aphids.

For fungicide and bugs, use neem oil.

Nature: I have found that there is now an ecosystem balance in my yard, and when the aphids came, so did the ladybugs, so I didn't even have to spray my soap solution. The healthier the soil is, the more mulch and proper conditions without the use of pesticides contributes to the good that overcomes the not so good.

Plant your trees in early fall or spring so they have time to adjust before harsh cold or hot summers. Watch videos on planting. Don't plant too deeply or you will smother the root ball. Don't add fertilizer and such for a long time. Just plant trees in soil, and maybe add compost if soil is depleted. Water and add mulch all around.

Trees need to be watered well a few times a week during hot summers the first few years. As they get bigger and the roots go deeper, they need less watering.

Seedling Care

I have the best luck with seedlings. I saved some book royalty money and purchased a $60 greenhouse at Home Depot. It was the best money I ever spent. I start everything in there if I can.

Grow starts in larger pots so you don't have to keep transferring them to larger and larger pots. Keep the soil damp, but not soaked.

When you see the first leaves, water then feed with vitamin B1 or fish emulsion mixed with water. Make sure the solution is super weak. If the label instructs you to add 1 tablespoon to a gallon of water, use a teaspoon instead. Feed weekly. When you are getting ready to plant your seedlings, bring them outside each day for a little bit to harden them. Do this for one hour the first day, then two hours, half a day, almost a full day, and so on, for a week.

If you can't afford a greenhouse figure out how to build one with sheets of plastic cover and an old tent. If that isn't something you can do, just set up tables in front of sunny windows and do it indoors.

Save all your food containers for pots: yogurt, sour cream, salsa, etc. Punch holes in the bottom. You can even use milk, tofu, and soy and almond milk containers.

Go online and look up the hardiness zone for your area, then look up a planting guide and print and post it on your refrigerator. It will tell you what to plant and when, and if you can plant in the ground as a seed or if it must be a seedling.

In order to cleanse, heal, and nourish the depleted soil, you may need a couple of years of growing things like sunflowers and beans, adding manure, compost, and coffee grounds. Sometimes soil is very depleted from years of being a lawn with chemical fertilizers added or it may have other lead, metals, and chemicals in it.

YOU CAN CLEAN AND HEAL THE SOIL. You just need to plant things that pull toxins out of the soil for a year or more. In Detroit, Michigan where they are dealing with soil polluted with all sorts of toxins and metals, they plant sunflowers and such to draw the metals and pollutants out. I don't know how many years they do this but eventually you can grow in the soil again. *Urban Roots* is a great documentary about the urban farmers in Detroit. Here is the trailer, but you can easily find the full documentary online, if interested: https://www.youtube.com/watch?v=wpifS2GV660

General Tips

If you have clay, sand, or hard soil use mulch, mulch, and more mulch. It breaks down and makes new soil. Keep adding things. Mulch, straw, manure, compost, etc.

Save milk jugs for watering and to use as bigger containers.

Save tin coffee cans and whatever other can you'd like to use as planting pots and to plant herbs.

Learn how to save seeds. We tried planting trees from seeds but it's far more complicated than I'd guessed. Right now we have a big, healthy avocado tree as well as many babies from seeds but I hear it takes years and years to bear fruit, and most of the time it isn't that good.

Learn to rotate crops and learn what plants are compatible and what plants aren't. Examples: onions and potatoes don't grow well together (despite tasting oh so good together). Artichokes suck up a lot of nitrogen so only beans, cabbage, and tarragon grow well with it. Sister plants are corn, beans, and squash. They grow well together and you can train the beans up the corn stalks and let the squash grow between the rows.

If you only have a patio and small strip outside the front door, do lots of container gardening. You can grow lettuce, tomatoes, herbs, potatoes, and more. You would be surprised at what you can grow and how much, once you master it.

Plant lots of flowers around the edges to attract bees.

Making compost is very simple but made fancy and complicated by many blogs and videos. All you need is a spot where you can dig a shallow hole measuring approximately 4 ft by 4 ft and 1 ft deep. You throw all your kitchen and garden scraps in it, layer with some dirt, leaves, and lawn clippings, and keep layering. Once you have a thick layer, you wet it to make it damp. Cover with a tarp and let it cook. Repeat.

We have two compost piles. One is in an old, raised garden bed filled with scraps, dirt, leaves, and lawn trimmings. The other one is just a pile behind the garage. It used to be a huge pile of horse manure that we had cooking, but we've since spread the manure on all our gardens. Afterward, we just started throwing the bucket of scraps and such out there and we continue to build the pile. Soon, we will also cover that one to let it cook.

There are things you **can't** put in the compost. These include citrus, avocado skins, any seeds, fast food, junk food, processed food, meat, dairy, and any feces other than chicken, cow, or horse.

Things that are **good** for the compost include any fruit and vegetable scraps, coffee grounds, tea leaves, banana peels, eggshells, leaves, and grass trimmings.

In time, you can add garden hoes, rakes, wheelbarrows, and trowels to the shed or garage. When I didn't have a trowel, I used big ol' spoons from thrift stores.

This year, I grew enough tomatoes in my new front yard kitchen garden to make 20 quarts of spaghetti sauce. That is inspiring. At the time of writing, nearing October of 2019, we are still eating plenty of eggplant and bell peppers from our harvest.

Chapter 7

Decorating Your Grown-Up Dollhouse

Beds should be new. Upholstered furniture should be new, unless you know where it has been and who has used it. We want to avoid bed bugs and other issues.

Big Lots is a good place for sofas and mattresses, especially bunk beds, if you live in a small house and your kids share a room.

Everything else that can be washed, scrubbed, boiled, and sterilized is from thrift stores, estate sales, garage/yard sales and hand-me-downs. You can find great furniture as well as items to fix up your home at Habitat for Humanity ReStore, a non-profit organization home improvement store.

In my home, almost everything has been purchased at thrift stores or yard sales. Many were hand-me-downs, things that others were discarding, or gifts. This goes for furniture, clothing, kitchen tools, most of my children's toys, paintings, art, books, tablecloths, linens, towels, comforters, books, lamps, dishes, and much, much more. If you have a little bit of money to play with, I have always had fun at Cost Plus World Market. This is the place you go to get that colorful, shabby chic look without paying a fortune.

The only new things in our house are the faux King-size Posturepedic mattress, as well as two small bunk bed mattresses. There is also one large painting that I bought in my youth before I understood the joys of thrifting.

An ugly sofa can be covered with a $30 cover and made to look new. You can also use a quilt, lovely bed cover, and even a nice sheet, if done right. We were gifted an L-shaped, cream-colored sofa by friends of ours, and I knew that it had been kept clean and well-cared-for. They had no animals, and the only issue was that it had dirty covers that happened to be washable. I washed the covers, bringing them back to a lovely cream color, and quickly found that it didn't take long for the sofa to look filthy again, just from simple living. This is despite not letting my kids eat in the living room and being a no-shoes household.

To remedy this problem, I bought soft and lovely throws and fabrics along with a pile of colorful pillows, and covered the sofa in a way I had discovered while perusing an Architectural Digest magazine at my dentist's office. It's definitely a shabby chic look but it works for us.

An ugly house can be made into a charming cottage with paint and plants. When we first purchased our house, it was ugly and stained. Everything was painted a shade I like to call "old, dirty white," both inside and out. Today, each room is painted in lovely and warm colors, and the floors are made of sweet, worn hardwood.

You can see some before and after photos in this video:

If you buy an old house you may discover that you have hardwood floors hidden under ugly carpet. To make them glossy and golden again, try Rejuvenate Professional Wood Floor Restorer or Scott's Liquid Gold. It's much cheaper than sanding and lacquering. Also, sanding too much may thin and weaken old floors. Scott's Liquid Gold is quick and super cheap, but if you have time for a longer drying period, pay the extra money and use Rejuvenate Professional Wood Floor Restorer instead.

Paint your rooms in warm and light colors. Dark colors make them look smaller and a bit tacky. That is just my opinion, of course. However, if you just paint an accent wall in a dark red or a rich green, that would work well. As a bonus, you will need less paint, which in turn, saves money.

Drapes and area rugs add warmth and color. A good look (that I don't follow, but might someday) is having a solid color sofa or living room set and patterned area rug with colorful pillows.

For missing doors or to replace ugly sliders on closets, put up curtains and rods. They look so much better on closets and can add privacy to a room missing a door.

You can bring in all sorts of indoor house plants and even outdoor plants such as geraniums. I have a house full of plants that I started from trimmings.

A great YouTube channel to learn DIY decorating on a budget is *Olivia's Romantic Home*. She has a small, plain house that she turned into the most charming dollhouse. She does all of it herself and on a small budget. She buys old furnishings from flea markets and antique stores, and gets all of her supplies from Dollar Tree and discount stores.

Don't follow today's styles or trends. It is your house to nest, fluff, and feather into a home that suits you and your family. My home is just a large, grown-up dollhouse. When I was a child, I loved to make dollhouses out of cardboard boxes that I decorated with things made out of egg containers, strawberry baskets, acorn tops, and small milk cartons. At one point, my mother bought me a large, wooden Victorian dollhouse, but it was the plain, wooden kind that needed to be painted, wallpapered, and carpeted. Back then, most boutiques and gift stores sold antique dollhouse furnishings as well as dolls that had porcelain heads, hands and feet. I would purchase a little item each time we went. Over time I had a fully decorated dollhouse with a parlor and tea set.

That collection and dollhouse are long gone. Sadly, they were destroyed in a leaky garage. However, I have a life-sized one that I decorate in the same way. I collect paintings, rugs, pieces of furniture, and bedspreads here and there, whenever there is a little money in the purse for just that.

I had fun collecting for my Victorian dollhouse, but I think I had the most fun when my friend's older sister taught me how to make dollhouses and furniture from boxes and containers.

I had a subscriber write me and tell me a story a while ago. Her mother was a single, working mother and money was scarce for them. Her neighbor received a Barbie dollhouse for Christmas so her mother made her a dollhouse out of boxes and made the furniture, as well. She loved that dollhouse, and I get it. It's the handmade, slowly, and cleverly crafted things that we create that mean far more than just going out and purchasing something off a shelf, or ordering it with a few clicks of the cursor.

Play with your grown-up dollhouse and enjoy every inch of it. Paint it in colors you love, fill it with items and furnishings that make you smile, and hang art that takes you to your happy place.

Just play.

Chapter 8

Homemade House Cleaning

I had a close friend who passed away from an illness some years ago. I had known her since we were 15 years old. She got pregnant and married when she was 17, and I watched her tend to her home through many years of living on very little money.

Although she was poor most of her life and later struggled as a single mother of two, her house was always clean, tidy, and cozy. It didn't matter that her house was a bit funky with 80s carpeting, peeling linoleum flooring, and old, worn furniture. She would spread lovely tablecloths on the table and always had scented candles burning. Her grandmother's afghan blankets were folded nicely to cover stains on the sofa, the dishes were always washed and drying on the rack, beds where made, and floors swept and vacuumed. The house smelled good, and during the holidays, there was always a spread on the table from treasures that she purchased at the local Grocery Outlet.

Her home was fully decorated during the holidays, especially at Christmas. She would have an outdoor flag for each season and holiday, and candles to match. She did this all on an incredibly small budget.

Her home was welcoming and I learned a lot by observing her ways.

You don't need a new home or trendy furniture from IKEA. You don't even need much money to have a lovely home that others will enjoy and your family will take pride in. You just need to clean deeply and freshen up often.

A clean house that smells good is the best, but with children and pets, it isn't always possible. I work hard to keep the smells of three dogs, four people, and an old house at bay. This means shampooing my carpets a couple of times a year and washing floors and dog beds often. I bathe the dogs often as well, but two of them are quite big and I need a chiropractic adjustment every time. I have rescued every one of our beloved dogs. I say *I* because Bali has never been on board, although he ends up falling in love with them later. I made an agreement with the Universe that any future rescue dogs had to weigh less than 20 lbs., and sure enough, our little Dachshund came to us this summer. I'm thoroughly sold on the small dog. I can plop her in the sink and suds her up anytime. Walking her is a breeze, her bed washes easily, and she's cute as a button.

I own a lot of cleaning tools and apparatuses now, though not all are necessary. A good vacuum with attachments is fine. If you only have hardwood or linoleum floors, a broom will suffice. All you need are some rags, vinegar, Dawn dish soap, some baking soda, and you are in business!

But I like to complicate things. Here is what I have in my collection:

Tools

Broom
Steam mop
Bona microfiber mop
Cleaning caddy filled with a scrub brush, rags, steel
scrub pad, toothbrush, and sponges
Pile of more rags from old clothes and cloth diapers
Bucket

Cleaners

Ajax Powder Cleaner
Bar Keepers Friend Powdered Cleanser
Fabuloso All-Purpose Cleaner
Bleach
Homemade cleaners

If you want to make your own cleaners to save
money and reduce toxins, here is what you need in
your cleaning pantry:

Castile soap or a bar of Ivory soap
Washing soda
Borax
Dish soap
White vinegar
Baking soda
Rubbing alcohol
Essential oils for scents (optional)

Here are some recipes for laundry detergent and
household cleaning must-haves. I have found all of
these recipes and more on DIY sites,
wellnessmama.com, *realsimple.com* (has great stuff
and super easy to follow directions with photos), and

Window Cleaner

2 cups water
½ cup white vinegar
¼ cup rubbing alcohol
1 to 2 drops essential oils

Heavy Duty Scrub

½ lemon
½ cup borax

All-Purpose Cleaner (counters, appliances, refrigerator)

4 Tbsp baking soda
1 quart water

or

1 cup water
1 cup vinegar
(I add a bit of Dawn dish soap)

Heavy Duty All-Purpose Cleaner (walls, counter, bathroom)

1 tsp washing soda
2 tsp borax
2 ½ cups hot water
¼ cup castile soap
12 drops essential oils

Floors

2 gallons warm water
1 cup vinegar
½ capful of castile soap or dish soap

Sink Scrub

2 cups baking soda
1 squirt castile soap

Drain Cleaner

½ cup baking soda
½ cup vinegar

Add the baking soda and vinegar down the drain, plug and let sit for 30 minutes.

Remove plug.

Carefully pour boiling hot water down the drain until the sink is unclogged.

Repeat if necessary.

Dishwasher Soap

2 parts borax
2 parts washing soda
1 part citric acid (available at health food stores and www.amazon.com)
1 part salt

Furniture Polish

1cup olive oil
½ fresh squeezed lemon juice

Store-Bought Cleaners for Those of Us Who Are Lazy

Now, if you aren't into making cleaners but still want to save money, here are some cleaners to use; but they are somewhat toxic, as all cleaners will be. You really don't need a pantryful of products. Here are a few good ones to do all the housework.

Note: You can get nontoxic, biodegradable cleaners. They tend to be expensive, so I think that it's best to make your own if you go this route, especially if you have babies and/or pets.

Fabuloso

Love this stuff. It's around $3 for a gallon and lasts for a couple of years. It gives off a wonderful lavender scent and cleans wonderfully. It is for floors, counters, and windows.

Ajax

I use this for the bathroom toilet, tub, and all my sinks.

Bleach, any brand

I use this sparingly on cutting boards I use for meat. It also goes on the toilet, inside and out. I sometimes use it in laundry when the whites are tinged yellow. If and when you do use it, be sure to open your windows and store carefully. DO NOT let children and pets inhale. It is TOXIC. But when it comes to the toilet and meat on a chopping board, I feel it is the most effective.

Break-Up or Easy-Off Heavy Duty Oven Cleaner

You can find a nontoxic, homemade cleaner on sites such as *wellnessmama.com*. However, I find that there are times when the hardcore stuff does the job for me. I just don't have kids around when I do it, and I do this intense oven cleaning only once a year.

Mr. Clean Multi-Surface Cleaner, Original Scent

All-purpose, cleans great, and smells great!

Murphy's Oil Soap or a lemon oil furniture polish

These polishes are great for cabinets and furniture.

Laundry Detergent: Roma (my favorite), Pinol, or Foca

The cost is about $5 and some change for a huge bag and it cleans and smells great. After much disappointment with other brands that were twice the cost, as well as with homemade detergent, I just recently tried Roma. I have a high efficiency (HE) washer that doesn't work too well, and not only were my clothes not getting clean, they smelled awfully bad. I found this detergent with with all the big bags of cheap detergent and decided I had nothing to lose. I'm very happy with it. Be careful though, powdered laundry detergents sometimes don't work well with HE washers as they are quite sudsy.

Laundry

As I mentioned previously, laundry is done every couple of days. I do try to reduce the washing as much as possible.

Each family member has a towel and uses it at least three to five times before washing. You are clean when you use it. Just be sure to hang it up so it can dry quickly and properly. I hang towels over doors or the shower curtain rod to dry quickly. It's when wet towels stay on the floor that they start to smell.

Change bedding once a week. Unless someone has wet the bed, there is no need to change it more frequently than that. We all bathe at night and are clean when we go to bed. My only issue is toast crumbs, jelly, and butter from when I let the boys eat breakfast in our bed while watching cartoons. You can be more or less strict. We just want to have a good time.

Clothes can sometimes be worn twice before washing. Jeans can be worn a couple of times. Pajamas can be worn a few times (if you bathe before bedtime). I have tops that don't get dirty or smell and I will wear them again.

Use the apron trick. I wear an apron most days and it keeps all kinds of stains and dirt smudges off my clothes. It's not just cleaning the house that gets me looking dirty, it's my children's hands on me that cause the blotches of dirt and food. Aprons save clothes.

My sons will usually wear their play clothes for a couple of days. They will wear their nice clothes when we go shopping or run errands and then I make sure that they take them off and change when we get home. If there was no eating, they are still fine.

Hang it up! Run a clothesline outside and have one of those collapsible laundry racks for indoors. Drying clothes naturally saves a lot of money in electric and gas bills and it saves your clothes, big time. The heat really wears them out. If nothing else, at least hang your delicates, underwear, and socks. I used to have a huge outdoor clothesline when we lived on the farm, and I loved it. Currently, I do use a dryer during the colder months and have found that if I put it on mild heat, it's easier on the clothes. Don't use regular or high heat with the dryer. I was having a lot of issues with ripped pants and was informed that it was due to drying my clothes on high heat.

Stains

There are two ways to do it. The homemade way is from *tidymom.net*. She calls it Miracle Cleaner and says it works on everything.

1 part blue Dawn dish soap
2 parts 3% hydrogen peroxide

And for those of you that don't want to make it...

Spray 'n Wash Pre-Treat Laundry Stain Stick. I've tried many and this is the best.

Rub all stain removers on clothes. Use an old toothbrush for tough stains. Let it sit for some time before washing. It's best to get the stain remover on stains immediately, if possible.

Separating laundry is good, too. Whites and lights in one load. Darks in another. I am a bad laundry lady. I only separate towels and washcloths, and I wash rugs separately and last. After washing dirty floor rugs, I run the washer with detergent to get it clean.

Hand wash delicates and undergarments if you want them to last. Hang them outside or over the shower rod to dry. Dryers wear out underwear fast.

Bleach is great for whites. Wash a load with a cup of bleach.

Vinegar is a great fabric softener and makes clothes cleaner and brighter. Add to the fabric softener dispenser tray. I have also taken to adding a half cup of baking soda before I put the clothes in. It really freshens the load.

Here are 3 different homemade laundry soap recipes. I have tried two of them and will be trying the other soon. People love these recipes.

Janie's Best Laundry Detergent Recipe

Here is her video if you want the full tutorial: https://www.youtube.com/watch?v=pm8D1eJ6Fms&t=4s

I loved this one for a good year but the next time I made it, I didn't follow directions. I used too much per load and it was too concentrated. My clothes became gray and smelly. It is imperative to mix it and water it down properly and NOT use too much.

You will need:

Five-gallon bucket with lid
Wooden spoon (just for the detergent)
Zote soap (400g bar or three small bars)
3 cups borax
3 Tbsp vegetable glycerin (NOW brand)
3 cups washing soda
1 cup baking soda
1 cup oxygen cleaner (I use OxiClean)
A laundry scent/fragrance booster (I use lavender scented Purex Crystals)

Directions

Grate Zote by hand (painful) or in a processor.
Simmer on low in a pot full of water until dissolved.

Add borax and stir until thick.

Fill 5-gallon bucket half way with hot water and add the Zote and borax mixture.

Add washing soda. Keep stirring.

Add more hot water to reach just a few inches from the top and keep stirring.

Add baking soda.

Add oxygen cleaner.

Add scent of your choice.

Add vegetable glycerin.

Fill the rest of the bucket with more hot water, until it

reaches about one inch from the top. All this time, you stir, stir, stir.

Let the bucket sit overnight.

The next day you will need to stir and break up the chunks.

Then, fill a gallon jug half way with the mixture and the other half with water and shake well before using for a wash.

It takes about half a cup for a full load. I would just leave the bucket by the washer and fill a gallon jug when I needed more. Each jug lasted a month for us. The whole bucket can make ten to twelve gallons. The cost is something like $1 or less per gallon.

Like I said, just follow the directions. When I made it properly, I loved it and my clothes were very clean.

Laundry Detergent (good for all washers)

Ingredients

½ cup Arm & Hammer Super Washing Soda
½ cup borax
¼ cup baking soda
1 bar grated soap (I like Zote)

Directions

Mix and store in small container.

Use 3 tablespoons per load.

I try to make several batches at once, or I find myself constantly making it.

Mary Hunt's Laundry Detergent Recipe

https://www.everydaycheapskate.com/food-and-recipes/a-little-update-on-my-favorite-laundry-detergent/

1-gallon jug with lid
¾ cup borax
¾ cup washing soda
¾ cup blue Dawn dish soap
Water

Add borax, washing soda, and 3 cups of water to jug.

Shake well.

Fill with more water, being sure to leave several inches at the top, adding Dawn dish soap last so as to not over bubble.

Mary uses ¼ cup per load in an HE washer with hard water.

It may vary depending on where you live and what kind of water you have.

Baby Laundry Detergent

This is great for infants and delicate skin.

Ingredients

6 cups washing soda
3 bars castile soap (Kirk's Natural Castile Soap is a popular choice)

Directions

Grate and store.

Use 1 to 2 tablespoons per load.

Don't add anything else. This is safe for baby skin or anyone with very sensitive skin.

Extra Tidbits for Keeping a Clean House

My biggest advice would be to have a no-shoe policy. Have a basketful of thick socks and slippers by the door for guests who go into shock because they have to remove their shoes. I hung a pretty sign on the outside of the door that reads, "Please Remove Shoes Before Entering." I was tired of asking and was surprised to find that some people put up a little fight. Shoes are gross and track in even grosser things. My children live on the floor and sometimes eat off the floor, literally (not something I encourage, but I'm learning that boys do strange things). I caught my eldest licking ice cream off the kitchen floor once. I keep them very clean.

Try to keep your house smelling good. I used to use Glade Plugins, but they would get too strong. Now I like to use a scented wax warmer or scented candles. Sometimes I use incense. I have a drawer full of these "good smell tools," as I like to call them.

If you want nontoxic, buy soy candles and scented waxes. You can even make your own if you'd like. Save candle jars and order wax or soy wax, wicks, essential oils, and candle dye, and you can whip up a batch quickly and easily. They have candle making supplies at craft stores such as Joann and Michaels, and recipes can be found online or in books at your local library.

For a quick air freshener, I love this homemade Febreze recipe. I like to spritz our furniture and throw pillows lightly before guests arrive.

Homemade Febreze

Spray bottle
1 ½ cups warm water
1-2 Tbsp baking soda
¼ cup liquid fabric softener

Add all to spray bottle, give it a good shake, and it's ready to use.

Another option is to have a pot of water on the stove simmering during the day. Just add lots of water and add your favorite spices for scents. Cinnamon, nutmeg, and cloves work great. Be sure to keep an eye on the stove to avoid any fires as the water evaporates. Alternatively, you can add these ingredients to a slow cooker set to low. It works amazingly, especially during the holidays.

Cleaning Schedules

Here are my daily, weekly, and monthly schedules. I have even included the seasonal schedules as well as a quick 30-minute tidy for when those unexpected guests visit.

I want to make this very clear — **I don't clean like this all the time.** There are times that I have lazy days, sloth-like days, and house cleaning burnout. This is just a nice schedule to keep us *sort of* on track.

Daily

- Make beds
- Cooking
- Wash dishes, clean kitchen counters (this goes on all day)
- Sweep kitchen and dining area
- Tidy house
- Take out garbage (doesn't need to happen daily)
- Give the toilet a quick scrub

There are also other things I do each day such as laundry, baking, gardening, organizing, or cleaning out closets and drawers.

Weekly

- Clean bathroom
- Vacuum whole house (with three dogs, I do this several times a week)
- Shake out all throw rugs outside
- Mop whole house
- Change bedding
- Dust
- Clean all mirrors
- Sweep patios, porches, front steps, and paths
- Change bathroom towels out for fresh ones
- Disinfect door knobs

- Wipe down appliances
- Wipe down dryer and washer
- Sweep garage (if your washer and dryer are out there)
- Scour kitchen sink, stove, and counters
- Organize cabinets, closets, and drawers (this is really over a period of months and more like a project)
- Laundry
- Weekly grocery shopping (this can be monthly or every two weeks)
- Water house plants (sometimes this is done monthly as I have mostly Ivy-type plants)

Monthly

- Sweep out cobwebs
- Vacuum and mop under furniture (such as sofas and beds, if possible)
- Wipe doors, walls, and light switches
- Wash shower curtain
- Wash all throw rugs (if you can)
- Wipe down kitchen chairs
- Wipe down window sills
- Clean ceiling fans
- Decluttering or organizing project

Beginning of Month

I like to not only clean, but also plan for my kitchen cafe.

- Wash out refrigerator and freezer in preparation for month's shopping
- A deep and thorough house cleaning

- Write out budget to keep on the path and make a grocery envelope
- Pay bills (I use online bill pay and auto pay)
- Plan menu for the month (you can do this weekly, also)
- Big grocery shop (I buy the bulk of our groceries monthly)

I change things around all the time. I used to do laundry only once a week, but now I have an HE washer that only uses the water it needs, so I do laundry every couple of days.

In order to get in the mood, I like to brew a strong cup of espresso or a pot of percolator coffee and listen to good ol' music from Pandora on our Smart TV. Sometimes I just listen to seminars on spirituality and Science, or educational videos on topics I'm inspired by.

Seasonal Chores

Twice a year, I wash all the windows (that's a lie; I wash outside windows once a year, if forced) and shampoo the area rugs (this is true, I am always eager to shampoo rugs). I do love when my windows are sparkly clean, though it doesn't last. I wash all comforters and pillows, along with mattress covers. Before and after winter, furnace filters are changed out, fire alarm batteries are checked, and gutters are cleaned out.

In the fall, I put all summer clothes in bins and store them in a closet or in the garage. I get out thick blankets and comforters for the beds, and throws for the sofa and recliner. When we had thin windows we would put up thick curtains.

In the spring, we put all the fuzzy, thick stuff away, get out cool blankets and clothing and everything else goes into storage, on closet shelves, or in bins.

Just before summer and winter, I set aside a day to go through the boys' clothes and sort out what is outgrown, too stained and torn (even for play clothes), and make sure they have a proper wardrobe for the upcoming season. This is especially true for the winter as they attend school in the forest and they need rain and snow gear to keep warm and dry.

Let's Go Out Into The Yard!

Garden Tips

Don't forget the yard and garden. This past summer, we pulled out the fancy barbecue grill that has been housing mice and spiders for years. I set up a table and chairs, brought out some umbrellas, and voila! We had an outside kitchen and dining room. We grilled chicken, barbecued corn on the cob, and ate outside until the summer was too hot and the flies became a nuisance.

With a long table and benches or old chairs you have a place for kids to do crafts, art, or clay projects outside. You can serve lunch after gardening and just make it an outdoor living day. I like to sweep and wash down with a hose often because food gets spilled and it gets dirty.

Weed Killing

You can use vinegar and hot water (compliments of

Penny Pinching Mama). Just pour on the weeds. This is great because you aren't poisoning the children or pets, not to mention the earth and air. Roundup is linked to all kinds of hideous diseases and cancers, and more are being revealed often.

Some motherly advice and extra tips for an easy life of clean:

Don't get crazy about having a perfect home. If you do the basics, make the beds, keep the kitchen sink empty, counters wiped, floors swept, and laundry put away, your house will be easy to maintain. Don't worry about what I like to call, "busy mess." Kids play, people play, and the house looks busy. That's a good thing.

Also, try to combine a chore with a routine. Here are some examples of how I do it:

-Oftentimes, while my boys are taking their bath, I will clean the sink and toilet.
-In the morning, while I wait for my coffee to brew, I empty the dish rack.
-When the boys are outside playing and I want to keep an eye on them, I sweep, weed, water the garden, and clean up the patio.
-When I take the boys to the library and park, we swing by the store and do some shopping.

Combine and multi-task. Today, I made Annie's Macaroni & Cheese and swept and mopped the kitchen while waiting for the pasta to boil. I make the bed and get dressed while waiting for toast to pop up from the toaster. Multi-tasking will save you time, time, time!

A big, big bit of advice — when cooking, always clean as you go! As pots begin to boil and sauces begin to simmer, you do the dishes, wash the counters, and clean out the sink. When the meal is ready, you will only have a pot or two and some dishes to clean up.

The 30-Minute Tidy

Here is a fun and quick way of pulling the house together within minutes. This is for the unexpected guest or grandparent visit, or just to do a quick straightening up before your husband gets home. You can even do it just for yourself.

- Throw every pot, pan, and dish in the dishwasher. Go through the whole house and collect glasses and dishes.
- This is where baskets in every room serve you well. Throw all toys, clothes, and books in the baskets and put into closets.
- Wipe down coffee table and dining or kitchen table and straighten up.
- Fold blankets or throws in living room and throw over sofas and recliners.
- Throw sheets and covers over beds and give a quick straighten or tuck. If it's guests that are coming, just close all the bedroom doors and don't worry about it, unless it's a room that will be seen for whatever reason. If that's the case, then make the bed and throw everything in baskets and put in the closet.
- Run the vacuum in main noticeable areas.
- Take wipes or wet cloths and wipe down sink in the bathroom that may be used by guests. Throw all the stuff that's sitting on the counter into a drawer. Hang towels neatly and give the toilet a scrub and let the

detergent sit.
- Spray some homemade Febreze everywhere.
- Light a big, scented candle in the kitchen. I love the candles that smell like baked cookies and pies.
- Brew a pot of coffee. The aroma is yummy and says, "I've been so productive. It's coffee break time!"

I must have a tidy house (I don't mind some toy mess) just to be able to think clearly. This may be neurotic, but I feel mentally balanced. I feel inspired to tackle other tasks when there is a semblance of order. However, there are days when I really can't do the whole song and dance of house cleaning.

Kids' Toys

When I had a dishwasher, I would lay screen fabric (the kind that goes in windows) down on both racks and fill it with the plastic toys. I would run it with soap and hot water to clean and disinfect them. I did this a lot when I had a daycare as it helped keep the toys clean and sanitized.

Now I just fill up the sink with very hot water and Dawn dish soap, add the toys and soak, rinse well, and air dry.

With stuffed animals and favorite blankies, you need to throw in the washer now and then on hot and use the dryer to finish disinfecting. Be sure to put them in a garment bag to help them keep their shape.

Chapter 9

Homemade Beauty

I'm going to add many recipes from my book, *The Homemade Housewife*. However, I will be honest: there are only 3 things I use daily.

- Corn meal as an exfoliant
- Ivory soap for my face
- Coconut butter on face and body

In the winter, I do use retinol and a glycolic peel. I order both products from www.amazon.com. The retinol is a 2.0% formula. For the glycolic peel, you'll want to start out with something very mild like 30% and move to a stronger formula slowly. Please use caution and read directions when using both, especially the glycolic peel.

Caution: do NOT use in the summer, if you are going outside often and for long periods of time, and always use a very strong sunscreen, or you will burn you face!

I always use a very strong sunscreen when outside, even when I drive. I tend to use sun hats and sunglasses when working outside as well. I wish that I had been this diligent years ago.

Exercise, eating a healthy diet with lots of fresh, organic fruits and vegetables, drinking plenty of water, getting lots of rest, as well as staying away from smoking, sugar, junk food, drugs, and alcohol are key to natural beauty. But if you bake in the sun all is lost. I have parts of my body that rarely saw the sun and the skin looks like that of a 20-something-year-old. The parts that were always exposed and I never thought to wear sunscreen on have a lot of sun damage. Fortunately, in my youth, I wore a lot of foundation with sunscreen in it, and it saved my face.

Here are some natural recipes for masks, makeup, and oils. Most of these are from *www.wellnessmama.com.* She has a fantastic website filled with natural, chemical-free recipes, and advice for everything from makeup to home remedies for sick children.

Gentle Facial Scrub

½ tsp Epsom salt
Cleansing cream

Face Mask (for oily skin and breakouts)

Ripe banana
1 Tbsp honey
10 drops lemon juice (fresh)

Apply to face.

Leave on for 15 minutes.

Rinse with washcloth and warm water.

Face Mask

1 egg yolk
1 Tbsp honey
Old-fashioned oats

Make a paste and apply to face. Leave on for 15 minutes. Rinse with warm water.

Coconut Oil Hair Mask

1 Tbsp coconut oil
1 tsp grapeseed oil
½ tsp lemon juice (for blond hair)

Heat until warm to touch and add lemon juice (blond hair only).

Apply to damp hair.

Wrap cling wrap and warm towel around head.

Wait 20 minutes, wash and condition.

Sugar Body Scrub

1 cup brown sugar
1/3 cup olive oil
1 tsp vanilla extract

Epsom Salt Scrub

For feet:

2 cups Epsom salt
¼ cup petroleum jelly
essential oils

For body:

2 cups Epsom salt
¼ cup olive oil or coconut oil

Face Wash

¼ cup castile soap
¼ cup brewed chamomile tea
¾ tsp olive oil
Several drops vitamin E oil
8 drops essential oils

Face and Body Lotion

Coconut oil/butter
Shea butter (for face)

Natural Microdermabrasion

Baking soda

Wet face.

Using fingertips, apply baking soda.
Massage face for approximately 3 minutes.

Rinse.

Shampoo

½ cup coconut milk
½ cup castile soap
20 drops essential oils
½ tsp olive oil or almond oil

This will keep for 1 month.

Shake before each use to mix ingredients.

Hair Rinse

One part apple cider vinegar
One part water

After shampooing, add about ⅓ cup of mixture to hair and leave in.

It makes hair shiny and cleaner.

Now, for those of you who are really, really ambitious and natural, here are some makeup recipes:

Natural Foundation (similar to powdered mineral makeup)

2 Tbsp zinc oxide
1 Tbsp arrowroot powder
1 tso gold mica dust
½ to 1 tsp natural clay powder
1 tsp finely ground cocoa powder or bronze mica powder

Mix until you reach desired shade.

Bronzer/Blush

Arrowroot powder
Cocoa powder
Cinnamon

Mix to desired shade.

For blush, add red or pink mica powder.

Eye Shadow

Cocoa powder (brown)
Spirulina (green)
Arrowroot powder (light)

Mix in arrowroot powder with either color, until desired shade has been reached.

Eyeliner

Cocoa powder mixed with coconut oil

or

Activated charcoal with whipped shea butter

Mascara

¼ tsp black mineral powder
¼ tsp bentonite clay
⅛ tsp vegetable glycerin
¼ tsp aloe vera gel
5 drops lavender essential oils

Lipstick

1 tsp beeswax pastilles
1 tsp shea or cocoa butter
1 tsp coconut oil

For color:

Add natural red food color or beet root powder for RED.

Add cocoa powder, cinnamon, or turmeric for BROWNS/TANS.

Place in heat safe jar.

Place in saucepan and bring to a boil.

Remove from heat and add desired color.

Store in lip makeup container.

So, there you go. It can be all natural and homemade, or you can find some good products at the store. I do half and half. I love the shampoo and rinse, because the chemical shampoos caused some problems with my scalp. I also make my own face wash, masks, and scrubs. I am not ambitious enough to DIY my makeup (yet).

Ivory soap and cornmeal are two other tricks I learned from my mother. Ivory soap can be used as face soap (as well as your homemade laundry detergent), and cornmeal is a great exfoliator for the face and body.

Chapter 10

100 Ways to Stretch the Budget

You know those little goofy things we see frugal people do? How about the things we saw our grandmothers doing that we thought were useless? They add up big time. The more money saving techniques you add to your daily and monthly routines — no matter how small, the more your savings will grow. Your paycheck will last the whole month and not just into the 3rd week. As the struggle of living paycheck to paycheck seems to disappear, you begin to see that it's true.

We don't struggle at all. Back when I was in debt, I used to. However, since the moment I paid it all off, I was determined to live a new lifestyle financially, especially when Bali and I married. That's not to say that I don't love to shop and blow money, or go out to dinner and a movie; but these are luxuries now, and we only do them when we have extra cash in the budget.

Currently, we have a huge goal to buy another property and to pay off our outstanding mortgage. These are big goals but completely doable if we get hardcore about the budget.

We are doing "no extra spending" months. It's easier to go month by month so we don't freak out. Here is what we are doing:

We are only paying the mortgage, utilities, gas for cars, and groceries. Nothing else. I try to keep the utility bills down, drive only long distances, and walk when weather permits. I keep working on our grocery budget to make it smaller without sacrificing on healthy foods.

I'm rereading *The Complete Tightwad Gazette* as well as other frugal and money saving books for inspiration and to be reminded of all the tips and tricks. I listen to other women who comment on my channel and glean great advice from them.

Here is a list of many things I do that I've learned from friends, family, *The Complete Tightwad Gazette,* other books about frugality, wise men and women, blogs, YouTube, and personal experience.

For pet food, I mix a bag of really inexpensive, but fairly good dog food with a high-quality brand. I used to mix Diamond Naturals Dog Food with Taste of the Wild Dog Food. Now I'm using Victor brand as my hound seems to be allergic to everything. I love giving our dogs treats, so I buy cheap Milk-Bone Biscuits and keep them in a cookie jar. I go to La Superior Supermercados, a grocery store, and buy cheap meat bones, boil in a huge pot of water, and add the bone broth to their morning food. Bone broth is very cheap to make and so good for them, especially when they get older. I do feed the stray neighborhood cats, as they keep the rodents and rats out of my gardens. I just buy a huge bag of Diamond Naturals Cat Food that lasts me half the year.

Hang a clothesline in your backyard or patio and never use the dryer again. All you need is a clothesline rope. The regular rope with stretch too much. It saves money *and* your clothes, big time.

Rearrange your furniture occasionally for a fresh and new look. Sometimes I rearrange my whole house, including rugs and paintings. This saves money as I get a fresh, new look, which makes me less likely to buy new things at the thrift store to decorate with.

Cheap rag rugs cozy up a kitchen. I get great ones at WinCo Foods for $5.

Save glass and plastic jars from pickles and mayonnaise to use as storage for nuts, raisins, coffee, sugar, and things purchased in bulk. I used to buy the huge pickle jars. I love those for storing flour, oats, and beans on the counter.

Use yogurt and cottage cheese containers and any other plastic container with a lid as your food storage containers.

Save little jars to store spices and herbs that you grow and dry or get at the bulk section of your grocery store.

Save old shirts, towels, and socks for cleaning.

Make small kitchen towels out of an old, big towel, if you are handy at sewing.

Make a sewing kit using an old cookie tin or Christmas tin. Add thread, scissors, needles, and whatever else you use to sew. You can even keep seamstress measuring tape, crochet needles, and much more inside.

Find an old percolator. They make great coffee and you will never buy filters again.

Use old wash cloths for dish sponges. Just throw them in the laundry when they start to smell badly.

Use candlelight at night when you're settled in to watch TV. Turn off all those money sucking lights.

A movie on TV and a big bowl of popcorn is a great way to have Family Night Friday.

I love libraries. You can get books (even new ones), music, the latest movies, and magazines, all for FREE. Wi-Fi is also available, for those of you who just canceled your Internet service. They even have computers to use if you don't have that luxury, either. There are great programs including story time for kids. Some libraries will have free movie and popcorn nights for families.

Throw a potluck at your home. Everyone brings a dish.

At garage sales, stock up on dishes, cutlery, and cloth napkins, and never buy paper plates, plastic cutlery, or paper napkins again. This is sustainable, green, environmentally conscious, and you will have plenty of settings for those potlucks you're going to start throwing.

Volunteer. It is free, fun, and community oriented. It shows a love and compassion for your fellow brothers and sisters who need a meal or some extra care. You can plant trees, feed the homeless, or hold babies at the hospital. It is a feel-good gift that keeps on giving. Get the teens involved so that they learn about community spirit instead of drugs and gang membership.

Public pools are cheap during the summer. Maybe you have one at your apartment. Hang out poolside with the little ones, or just by yourself with a book. Pretend you are on vacation.

Go to McDonald's and let the kids play at the indoor PlayPlace on rainy days. Buy cheap ice cream cones or a couple of value menu items for all of you as a treat.

Buy decorations for birthdays and holidays at thrift stores. Get the kind that last for a while and just pack away in boxes when not in season. You can build up your collection over time.

Decorate during the holidays. You may not have money, but decorating makes you feel rich and in good spirits. Don't buy gifts. Instead, bake homemade sugar cookies (the most cost effective and easy) and collect tins and baskets at the thrift stores. A tin of homemade goodies is far more touching than a gift someone will just have to put away in a closet.

Invest in an artificial Christmas tree. You will have a tree every year and not have to worry about being able to afford the real thing.

Listen to free holiday music on the radio.

If you see someone's plants dying and they have no interest in them, offer to adopt. I have a lot of indoor and outdoor foliage thanks to the "Adopt an Almost Dead Plant" mission.

The radio is free and there are a lot of great stations. You can listen to classical while you read, hip hop as you clean, rock out as you declutter, or listen to the news, if that's your thing. I don't actually recommend this.

Have a friend over for coffee. Make a batch of those homemade biscuits. This is real living and loving.

Go to parks and forest preserves. Get a park pass for the year and explore.

Go to free beaches and forests.

Walking is free and enjoyable. Explore your neighborhood and your town.

Take a book to the laundromat. Enjoy the mini break. Have a friend join you and catch up.

Have pancake mornings every Saturday to make it special. I buy the huge bags of Krusteaz pancake mix. It only requires water and lasts for months and months. It's a cheap way to make the weekend special for kids and adults alike!

Start a book club.

Start your own self-help group. Meet once a week or month and work from a book that is about self-reflection and healing. You can get the book at the library. Have everyone bring a baked good and you brew the coffee or tea.

Start a blog. It can be free in the beginning, and then $8 per month if you start wanting to do something bigger with it.

Start writing a book. You can self-publish on www.amazon.com for free. Marketing, promotion, book covers (even creating paperbacks and ebooks) can all be done for free online. You can become a published author for free!

Spring clean, fall clean. Scrubbing the house can be so therapeutic and motivating. Put on a pot of coffee and some great music and get into it.

Order a big stack of books from the library for you and the kids and sit out in the yard near your new garden and read novels. We have new stacks and piles of library books every week.

Find a little side job cleaning a house or two, or walking a dog (or two). Get paid to organize someone's house, do their laundry, clean out a garage.

Learn to swap and barter. It's the new "in" thing.

Start your own daycare if you want to stay home with your children. If you just love kids and are great with them, this is also for you. It's easy and inexpensive to get started. There are programs out there that reimburse you for the cost of snacks and meals you provide. It can be a great little business that is also fun. I did it for some time when my husband was unemployed and it paid the bills, the rent, and the groceries. It was fun to build and run and it cost us very little to create.

Go back to school. You can take online courses or night classes at a local college. There are Regional

Occupational Programs where you can learn a trade at your own pace and for very little money. There are quick programs to get a certificate within six to nine months and start a new career! The Board of Governors Fee Waiver is a state program that will pay for your classes. Federal Student Aid will pay for your books. School can be free! Get an Associate of Arts degree, and then go on to a bigger college or university. Take a couple of semesters and become a dental assistant, veterinary assistant, nurse assistant, mechanic, secretary, or accountant. All of these can be accomplished in less than a year. You can even take computer literacy classes if you need help with that.

Go to YouTube and watch some Abraham with Esther Hicks. Learn about the Law of Attraction. We don't want to stay stuck, right? There are other spiritual teachers as well. Joyce Meyer for the Christian heart. Bruce Lipton, Dr. Joe Dispenza, and Gregg Braden for the science-meets-spirituality heart. Maybe even Tony Robbins?

Learn DIY crafting, car and house repair, decorating, cooking, baking, homesteading, child-rearing, sewing, knitting, fermenting, gardening... It is incredible what you can learn on YouTube! I homeschool myself all the time.

Give up any expensive habits such as smoking, drinking, marijuana, and/or drugs. You will never get ahead if you take part in any of these vices. They are detrimental to one's health, well-being, motivation, and wallet. Let's not forget their ability to turn your life into a real tragedy.

Homeschool. This can be free if you utilize the

library and Internet. Join a homeschool co-op. Some homeschool programs offered online or through schools will allot a certain amount of funds for your child to take classes and purchase books and supplies.

Make your own playdough. Doing so will provide hours of creative fun for kids and adults.

Start an arts and crafts box for the kids. It can be crayons, pens, coloring books from the dollar store, scratch paper, popsicle sticks, cotton balls, and old magazines for collages.

Make a dream board or dream box. All you need is a piece of cardboard or old box with lid, glue, magazines, and scissors. Decorate, be fun, and get creative. With the dream box, cover it in wrapping paper or pictures and fill it with wishes and dreams. It works.

Watch *The Secret*.

Create little sanctuaries throughout your home. I have feathers and crystals in my kitchen window. Beside them, I keep little old toys and rocks collected by my children, photos that make me smile, candles, and small plants. I create shrines in window sills and on dressers that remind me of what is loved, precious, and worth working toward. I display things that remind me of my beloved family and faith.

Adopt a pet from The Humane Society of the United States or your local shelter. For a small fee, it is spayed/neutered and has all its exams and vaccinations. If you were to pay for all of this yourself, it would be well into the thousands of dollars. Also, this is a loving and compassionate act. These shelters are overflowing and these animals need a loving home. Make sure that you get a pet your family and budget can handle. Cats require little and eat very little. If you are lucky, it may be an indoor/outdoor cat and you won't even need a litter box. We had a rescue cat that moved herself in and I have never had a litter box. She came and went as she pleased, and a big bag of $15 cat food lasted almost a year. She was already spayed so that saved us. If you choose a dog, you must be settled because if you must move, it is very hard and very expensive to find a home where dogs are allowed (even cats limit the choices). Dogs require a lot of love and walking. Be prepared, they are furry children.

Learn to sew or knit. You can make family clothes and/or Christmas gifts.

Cook everything from scratch. It's easier than you think and saves a ton of money.

Bake all your own bread.

Learn how to bake your own cakes for birthdays, weddings, and any special occasions. I found a channel called *Chelsweets* that makes it look easy: https://www.youtube.com/channel/UCjbZLZLPn1MZw0 5VkWxSf8g

Exercise can be free. Walk, jog. There are free workout videos online. In addition to yoga videos, there are lots of great fitness channels on YouTube. BIKINI BODY MOMMY and FitnessBlender are two good ones. There is your free home gym.

Borrow *The Complete Tightwad Gazette* from the library and read it all! There are tons of great ideas from so many wise women on how to make it on a few bucks. In the back of the book, around page 900, you will find many success stories. Read them when you need a boost.

Stretch the dish soap and shampoo by adding water. You can even water down store bought laundry soap.

Start a change jar with all the loose change you find in your pockets, sofas, wallet, and car.

Spend a day with a friend and a thermos of coffee, and go from garage sale to garage sale in your neighborhood to find amazing deals. Keep a mental or paper note of what you desire for your home and family. Make it a treasure hunt!

Walk the dog daily or even twice a day so you both get out and about. Fido will love you!

Master couponing if you like. I just live on sales.

Reuse plastic bags from bulk foods for packing lunches, lining little garbage cans in the bathroom, or cleaning up doggy poop.

Create and build up a surplus food pantry. Anytime you see big, incredible sales on foods you use, stock up. Building up a good store of foods that are dried and canned is smart for those times when the grocery money doesn't stretch to cover the whole month.

Reuse disposable razors over and over and over.

If you are on The Special Supplemental Nutrition Program for Women, Infants, and Children (WIC), you get so many containers of juice. You can pour some in a glass and add a little ice water for a delicious and refreshing beverage. You can also make popsicles for summer treats.

Add frozen vegetables to all the dishes you make. It fills up the plates and doubles recipes. It's healthy and gets kids used to vegetables and eating well.

Grow your own houseplants from trimmings.

Buy a tea set from a thrift store. Have the ladies over for a tea party.

Find a used air popcorn maker, or use a big pot with lid to make your own. This is so much cheaper than microwave popcorn. It tastes far better, too.

Have an aloe vera plant for burns, sunburns, and cuts.

Start a garden.

Say goodbye to corporate banks that nickel and dime you and switch to a credit union.

Make soups out of leftover chicken and turkey carcasses.

Buy used cars or check out repossessed cars.

If you don't want to become vegetarian or plant-based, just try having a few vegetarian/plant-based dinner nights.

Save the casserole pans from frozen lasagnas and such to reuse for your own cooking.

Collect board games purchased at thrift stores and garage sales to play with family for a free night of entertainment and good, old-fashioned fun.

Turn down the water heater temperature.

Make your own iced tea. All you need is a big jar or pitcher, tea bags, and hot water. Cover and let it sit in the sun in your backyard or patio. When it has brewed, add ice and enjoy.

Use up old food. Bananas can become banana ice cream or banana bread and muffins. Old tomatoes can become sauce for pizza and spaghetti.

Make your own pizzas from scratch (including dough) instead of ordering out.

Make baby bibs from old shower curtains and towels.

Save all junk mail and use as fire starter if you have a wood stove.

Have a clothing exchange party.

Use old washcloths for baby wipes.

Nursing is free and cloth diapers are a one-time expense.

Oatmeal is the cheapest and healthiest breakfast

food.

Use kitchen sink for baby baths. If it's an infant, fold a towel and put in the bottom of the sink and use very little water.

Bring your own popcorn and candy to the theater and find deal days.

Buy a small, fixer-upper house.

Buy generic versions of food.

Make your own air freshener. A small pot of hot water on the stove with cinnamon sticks and cloves smell divine.

Save old clothes and make your own quilts. Use old sheets for the back of the quilt.

Try to put 10% or more of each paycheck into savings.

Have an emergency fund that covers at least six months of living expenses in case a job is lost.

On Valentine's Day, have your spouse bring you garden seeds or real plants instead of the bouquet that only lasts a few days.

Grind your coffee super finely. The finer the grind, the less you have to use when making a pot. My coffee lasts twice as long now.

Make your own candy.

Make moving cheap. Declutter and get rid of all the

junk before you pack. Get free boxes from grocery stores. Borrow a truck.

Reuse paper bags for wrapping gifts.

Invest $80 to $100 in a carpet cleaning machine and clean your own carpets seasonally or annually.

Reuse pumpkins from fall and Halloween decorations for pies, purees, and dog food. For dog food, you just steam and put in their kibble for a healthy snack.

Save all your vases and baskets from gifts and bouquets for decoration, storage, and so much more.

Use the juice from canned tuna and chicken and put it on the dog or cat's food. They love this treat.

Rent out a room. If you are handy and it's legal in your area, convert the garage, a shed, or upstairs portion of your home into an apartment. Some counties, such as Marin County, will pay you for this.

Chapter 11

Holidays, Guests, Travel, and Birthdays on a Budget

This is a section from my book *The Homemade Housewife*.

Holidays and birthdays can be so stressful and expensive, but they don't have to be. When you learn to do things wisely you can look forward to Christmas, or that birthday, and have fun without worrying about money.

Parties, Holidays, and Vacations on the Cheap

Here are a few tips to get you started:

- First, start a holiday envelope (sinking fund) that you put money toward every month just like all the other bills.
- Start shopping for the holiday right after the holiday (way after Black Friday, though). Sales are amazing right after Christmas and Thanksgiving because the retailer needs to get rid of leftover inventory. You can save up to 80% sometimes. So, buy the turkey, the canned cranberries, the stuffing, and store it (this is where it pays to have a deep freezer). You can even get an extra turkey or two and give to a less fortunate

neighbor or an elder on a pension.

- Hit the thrift stores after the holidays. They have the best decorations and sell for even less to clear it all out.
- After Christmas Sales: you can buy decorations, lights, stock up on baking supplies, and even some basic gifts.
- Have big tubs for storing your holiday, party, and gift wrap.
- Start a stationery tub. Fill it with the cards, tissue, wrapping paper in good condition, and gift bags you have collected.

Gift Stockpile

I have a big storage tub filled with gift bags, tissue paper, and blank cards. I have collected this for years. At every party of mine, I have saved the bags and tissue that was salvageable. Every time I see great cards for cheap, I stock up. Now, when there is a party, I have all I need, except for the gift.

There is a way to stock up on future gifts, also. When you are out garage sale shopping or thrifting and you see delightful items in great condition, you may think of someone in particular, or a future baby, bridal shower, or wedding. Get it and store it. When you're at discount stores and there is an incredible deal on infant wear or small household items that would be great gifts, buy them.

When you're at the thrift store (child- and husband-free) and see great clothes, toys, and other items that are in great condition, start Christmas shopping for your family early. Just make sure that you have a foolproof hiding spot in the house or garage. Do Christmas shopping in April! Stock up on toys for birthdays. A bit of scrubbing brings new life to thrifted toys.

This is such a great idea because when you are invited to a birthday party, baby shower, wedding, or any special event, you are prepared. You don't have to turn it down due to low funds.

Stock up on old tins and baskets, too. What a great way to give homemade cookies and treats during the holidays!

During Christmas, my kids get presents. Sometimes my husband and I will get some item we have wished for all year, but we do not buy gifts for others. Who has the money for that? What I do, is send cards with well wishes and bake cookies. I let the kids decorate them and hand those out to neighbors, the mail carrier, and other public servants and friends. People love homemade goods.

Birthdays

I'll be honest. I'm not crazy about birthdays. Not mine, not anyone's; but I do love making the day fun for my boys. I had a list of ideas in this section way before I had the birthday party down. I'm updating this because the last couple of years I found a way to have lovely parties without the drama and stress.

My son, Arjan's sixth birthday was the best. We only invited close family and friends. We cleaned the house well and picked flowers and roses from the front yard to fill vases for each room. I added the leaf to the kitchen table to make it longer and allow for more seating. I spread a lovely tablecloth on it. We cooked tons of food, both Indian and Mexican. It was all vegan as we were immersed in a plant-based lifestyle that year. We had a big spread and used all our dishes, utensils, and cloth napkins. Nothing was disposable.

I baked and decorated two huge cakes and added dinosaurs.

We bought Arjan a large and expensive gift (this was a lesson learned) as that was all he wanted, and Sammy got a gift as well. The boys both get gifts on each other's special day. We have always done this, and it's now a tradition.

There were no decorations other than the bouquet, music, and a table full of food, but it didn't matter because the boys had their family, as well as new toys. It was the best party.

We do this for everyone in the family now, except me. I always choose a meal at Sizzler and a good thrift store shopping spree.

Other Parties, Including Adult Birthday Celebrations

Potlucks are the way to go.

You can decorate your house with vases full of flowers from your yard, tea light candles, and some streamers for that extra touch.

I have saved all the vases from every bouquet of

flowers I've ever received from work, boyfriends, my bridal shower, and husband. You can also find cheap vases at thrift stores and garage sales.

Bake your own cake and decorate it with flowers. It looks fancy. Learn how to decorate a cake from watching videos on YouTube. It only requires a couple of tools and you can buy or make white frosting and then dye it different colors.

Chop up tons of vegetables. Celery and carrots are cheap. Make your own hummus; it impresses people and is very yummy. Make a platter out of fresh vegetables, olives, pickles, chips, crackers, and some dip.

Make huge casserole dishes or pans of enchiladas.

Make a fabulous playlist on Pandora with all your favorite music. Hook some speakers up to your laptop and let everyone enjoy the tunes.

Good food, music, and fun people are all you really need for a great party.

People always ask what to bring. Have them to bring a dish, or the wine and beer. You can save so much money this way.

Use real plates and silverware. Stock up on funky mismatched plates and utensils at garage sales if you throw a lot of parties. Stock up on cloth napkins. Plastic glasses, too. That way you never buy paper plates, napkins, plastic utensils and cups. That is a big cost and so environmentally wasteful. Others will be impressed with your green ways.

If it's an evening party, string white twinkle lights indoors and outdoors (if you have a yard). Have tea lights everywhere, along with big candles. This creates a very romantic and charming ambiance.

Make huge pitchers of ice water with mint leaves and lemon (or lime) slices.

You have just thrown a party for, literally, a few dollars. Congratulations!

Holidays

We love the holidays. Fall is one of my favorite seasons. There is so much to enjoy; the turning of the leaves, all the golds and reds lining the streets, the smell of crisp air that brings with it all the pumpkin picking on old farms, and family gatherings. It's the time of year that I indulge in those wonderful Hallmark Christmas movies. Then there are the lovely Christmas carols and the way that baking sugar cookies in such large quantities make the house smell like butter and sugar for days…

There are frugal and easy ways to do holidays. You can look like you really go all out, but in actuality, you put very little effort into it.

Fall

In the fall, we travel to farms and pick pumpkins of all sizes. I decorate our home with pine cones that we have collected from our trips to Lake Tahoe,

California, and fall leaves we collect on our walks. I place large pumpkins on our front steps and little pumpkins on our window sills. I bring out the orange, yellow, and red candles for effect.

We hang a flag for all the seasons and holidays outside our front door.

Make it a point to really enjoy the seasons. Take the kids out to explore, collect, and appreciate the turning of each season, and talk about what each one brings.

Thanksgiving

You can host this dinner or go to someone else's house. I like hosting because then we have tons of leftovers for later meals. You can find great sales on turkeys right after the big day, and I usually pick one up if we didn't host the celebration. You can work with this bird in so many ways.

If you host, take advantage of the buy one, get one free special most stores offer, and get that extra bird or ham.

Have everyone bring a dish.

Have your husband help with the cleaning and preparing.

You've already decorated with the fall leaves, pine cones, pumpkins, and candles, right?

Have one friend or family member come early that day and help with the cooking. Never cook Thanksgiving or Christmas dinner alone. The more you can get to help, the more it becomes fun, instead of overwhelming.

Have everyone help clean up.

Be generous when giving your guests leftovers to take home. The bird will keep you busy enough.

If you bought two birds, freeze the other.

With your leftover bird, you can make casseroles, turkey pies, and soup. Simmer the carcass with leftover vegetables and meat and make a stock to store in the freezer.

Christmas

I love, love this holiday!

Although we do not buy gifts for adults, the children get two toys of their choosing, and then I stuff their stockings with little toys and candies.

Hang your holiday flag and string your lights (or be like us and leave them up all year so you just have to plug them in, yay)! Get out those gold and red candles. We have an artificial tree and it's free every year. I love real, fresh trees and we do that when money is a little more abundant. I decorate the day after Thanksgiving, true to tradition.

On the day after Thanksgiving, I turn on those Christmas carols, pull out the boxes of decorations from the garage, and put up the artificial tree. I hang stockings (you don't need a fireplace for this) and the season begins!

We read Christmas books and Bible stories for children. I have the carols playing the whole month (this might make some of you crazy) and I indulge in lots of holiday movies. I find that these days, there aren't many Christmas movies for children, so you may have to search online or Netflix.

You can create a holiday station with Pandora online. Of course, there is always that one station on the radio that will start playing carols in November.

I stock up on flour, sugar, and cooking margarine from discount stores such as Grocery Outlet. Thrift stores and dollar stores are great for baskets, holiday tins, and boxes for cookies. I have a few days on which I bake up a storm. You can just bake sugar cookies and then decorate them. You could also make homemade fudge and/or another treat we only make at Christmastime called "Christmas Crack" because it's so good and addictive (it's really called "Puppy Chow").

Sugar Cookies (source: www.allrecipes.com, courtesy of Jill Saunders)

Ingredients

1 ½ cups butter (or margarine, it's less pricey)

2 cups white sugar

4 eggs

1 tsp vanilla extract

5 cups all-purpose flour

2 tsp baking powder

1 tsp salt

Directions

In a large bowl, cream together butter and sugar until smooth.

Beat in eggs and stir in remaining ingredients.

Cover and chill overnight.

On a floured surface, roll out dough to desired thickness.

Using festive cookie cutters, cut out shapes.

In a preheated oven, bake for 6 to 8 minutes at 400 degrees Fahrenheit.

Cool and decorate!

These are great cookies.

Sugar Cookie Frosting (source: Safeway)

Ingredients

4 cups confectioners' sugar

½ cup shortening

5 tablespoons milk

1 teaspoon vanilla extract

Food coloring

Directions

In a large bowl, using an electric mixer, cream together sugar and shortening.

Add remaining ingredients and mix until just combined.

I put a glob in separate bowls and add all kinds of colors to decorate cookies.

This recipe is very easy and yummy.

Puppy Chow

Ingredients

18 oz box of any kind of Chex cereal, rice works best

½ cup peanut butter (whatever is cheapest, I usually use Jif)

1 cup chocolate chips

1 ½ cups confectioners' sugar

Directions

In a saucepan over low heat, slowly melt the chocolate.

Add peanut butter and mix until smooth.

Pour mixture over a big bowl of Chex cereal and mix.

Add powdered sugar to a large bag.

Add cereal mixture, close bag and shake until coated.

Fudge

Ingredients

2 Tbsp butter

1-12 oz bag of chocolate chips

1 can sweetened condensed milk

Choice of mix-ins (crushed nuts, candy, marshmallows, etc.)

Directions

In a medium saucepan, melt 2 tablespoons real butter and 1 bag chocolate chips on low heat, stirring constantly.

Add 1 can sweetened condensed milk.

Line a casserole pan with wax paper and put all kinds of goodies in the bottom (crushed nuts, candy, mini marshmallows, and coconut flakes are good choices).

You can choose just one, or mix and match as much as you want.

Pour chocolate and butter mixture on top and refrigerate until hardened.

Put them in a pretty tin or box. People love this! Thank your mail carrier, your doctor, hairdresser, family, friends, and neighbors. You will win hearts everywhere.

I also buy inexpensive cards at the dollar store and send one to everyone I know. It's fun.

If the kids request a special toy, they get one or two, depending on what it is and how much it costs. No electronics are ever included. I prefer toys that they can use to build and create. I stuff their stockings with fun little toys, games, and treats.

When kids are older, books and movies can be good gifts.

As for me and the man, well, sometimes there are some things we really want, and this is the time of year that we treat ourselves. For example, I gifted us a lovely quilt set for the main bed one year, and an Italian stovetop espresso maker another year.

New Year's Eve, Valentine's Day, Easter, and All Other Holidays

With these holidays, you just hang that flag and decorate with candles. Use gold and black for New Year's Eve/Day, red and white for Valentine's Day, and pink and blue (or any pastel color you find) for Easter. You can get decorations at thrift stores and dollar stores.

As for the dinners, you can invite people and make it a potluck. Remember, all it takes is good food, good music, and great friends and family.

Keep it simple. The decorations and music are what make it seem elaborate. You can stock up all year for these seasons and holidays.

I go to Grocery Outlet and the local dollar store for more decorations, candles, streamers, and cheap baking supplies. I'm sorry; I just don't have the cash to make organic sugar cookies this year.

If you have children, make sure and dye eggs for Easter and set up an egg hunt. Check with your town or city to see if they are having a community egg hunt. Those are lots of fun and usually free. Many times, they will also have face painting, games, and activities, as well. When I was a child, I loved getting an Easter basket loaded with goodies on that special day.

For Valentine's Day, make homemade cards for loved ones or send a special email. For a partner, do something nice. Cooking their favorite dish or pie is inexpensive and thoughtful. I really don't put much effort into this day. I figure that my Valentine's Day gift is having a great husband and two amazing children.

Halloween

One year, we made a huge mistake and went into an expensive store that specializes in Halloween costumes and decorations. I went wild and purchased all these cheap costumes and junk for a total of $300. Most of the junky lawn decor was either quickly ruined, or I got rid of because it gave me the creeps. The costumes we purchased were only worn once and the kids complained that they were too itchy.

Then, I drove by a yard that had an array of homemade decorations displayed and I knew what I had to do. The following year, Halloween only cost us a couple of dollars.

At a garage sale, I found over half a dozen of those fun scarecrows that people put in their gardens and yards in the fall. I grew my own pumpkins to decorate with. I only paid $1 for the seeds.

I'm not much for creepy decor. However, I did see a fun idea once. I saw a house that had the front yard decorated with huge pumpkins. They were made out of giant yard waste bags. How clever!

Another thing you can do is make simple ghosts to hang from your trees. Take a white cloth the size of a handkerchief, put a golf sized ball in it, tie it off with some twine or a rubber band, draw a simple face with permanent marker, and hang it up. This can also be accomplished by cutting up an old sheet and buying some inexpensive foam balls from a craft store or the dollar store.

Last year, instead of buying bags of candy for the boys and I to gorge ourselves on and be sick for days, we baked cookies and decorated them like pumpkins instead.

Locations for Parties

Parks are a great place to celebrate for free. They have tables and benches, fields and climbers for kids to play, and a barbecue grill or two. Setting up and cleaning up is easy out there. This is a great option for those of you who don't have a backyard or large house.

For big anniversaries and weddings, you can rent a local grange for a small fee. There is usually a kitchen where the party food can be cooked as well as a dance area where you can have a DJ.

Your own backyard with strung lights and streamers can create a fun scene.

The beach is great if you live near one.

Forest parks are another good choice.

You can celebrate at a friend or family member's house, if they have one big enough and they don't mind.

Being the Guest

If you love going to friends' homes for dinner, then stock up on good wines when you see a deal. A guest with a good bottle of wine in tow is always a welcomed guest.

Learn a couple of fun, easy, and yummy hors d'oeuvre or main dish recipes to take to a potluck.

Grow flowers to bring to others' homes.

Vacations

Vacations don't have to break the bank. Try road trips, going out of town to visit friends and family in other states, or camping.

When visiting out of town, make it fun and interesting by exploring the town and whatever special touristy things the town may offer. If it's the ocean, spend a day at the beach. If you're in Los Angeles, go to Disneyland or check out Hollywood. Anywhere you travel, there are always forts or trails, old buildings, and old parts of a town.

Pack food. Grab an ice chest and picnic basket, and load up on goods for the trip there and back. If you need groceries while in town, find a store that isn't too expensive. Buffets are inexpensive and with so many options, this choice is sure to please every family member's palate. Just be careful not to stay if it looks the least bit dirty or funky.

Camping is a very fun way to be together as a family and can be fairly cheap. Invest in a tent and sleeping bags if this is something you may do often.

We are very fortunate to have friends in Oregon near Ashland, as well as on the coast. All it costs is a tank of gas and some groceries and we have a vacation.

When staying with other people, I will bring groceries to make a dinner or two for all of us. I also help with washing dishes, cleaning the kitchen, tidying up after my boys, and making our beds. This way, our friends and family will be happy to have us around. It is important to be considerate and make it easy for them.

Having Guests for a Period of Time

This can be a money sucker, but not if you plan wisely.

First and most importantly, don't go out to eat! That is where the money goes. That, and shopping.

You can find lots of fun and free things to do for your guest/s, just look online or go to your community center and ask for activities that don't require money.

Go to farmers' markets. That's fun and social and you can get the groceries for the week.

Go to free museums or old churches.

Take long walks to exercise and catch up.

Create a lovely patio area with candles and plants where you and your guest/s can sit, sip coffee and eat toast in the morning, and sip tea and eat crumpets in the evening. Light the candles at dusk and enjoy wine and cheese. People love sitting outside and talking over a bit of pie or good iced tea.

Make your house cozy and charming so you all enjoy hanging out there and being together.

Put out spreads during the day and have a big casserole or pot simmering on the stove. My mother was a good hostess. We were also very poor, but she made our home very enjoyable for our guests. She would always have the person's favorite beer, wine, or drink. There was always good music playing, a bouquet of flowers on the table, and all kinds of foods spread out for everyone to just graze as they wished. There was also a pot of something delicious on the stove. Sometimes it was chicken and dumplings, other times it was spaghetti sauce to have with delicious pasta and a loaf of French bread heated in the oven and slathered with butter. You can even have a pot roast or hearty soup going in the slow cooker. Serve with freshly baked bread. There is nothing like the smell of homemade food simmering all day.

Take your guest/s to open forest preserves, parks, or beaches. Plan a picnic.

Rent good movies from Redbox or stream them on Netflix.

Remember, your friends and family are visiting because they want to be with you and your family. You don't have to throw a festival in their honor. Just feed them well and have fun.

Final Note

I hope you found this book helpful, or at least inspiring. I have many other books as well as a YouTube channel to give support and keep you motivated. I love talking about the home and learning to live on less so we have more time for family, friends, ourselves, our dreams and our children.

If you go to my Goodreads page, you will see a long list of books I've read and been inspired by, as well as a great list of fiction.

At this point, the list of books and channels would be too long for me to include here.

I look forward to hearing from you all.

Kate

Printed in Great Britain
by Amazon

41097409R00118